TAKE OFF THE MASK

BE YOURSELF

BY

DERRICK M. THOMPSON, SR.

DEDICATION

This book is dedicated to our new church family of The Solid Rock Community Church of God located at 1904 N. Michigan Ave, Kissimmee, Fl. 34744. To Bishop Whitfield D. Blenman our Pastor Emeritus and family; Rev. Dr. Matthew A. Quainoo our Senior Pastor and family.

To our former church family of Covenant Faith Church of God located at 10505 S. Halsted St; Chicago, IL. 60628; where Rev. Dr. E. Raymond Chin was the former Senior Pastor.

To my wife Isolyn, our children, Karen, Derrick, Jr (Arnetta); Duvol (Raquel); our grand-children, McKale; Kori Lynne; Parker Yve: and Graham Quinton.

♦♦♦♦♦♦♦♦♦♦♦

🙂 🙂 🙂 🙂 🙂 🙂 🙂 🙂 🙂

<u>TAKE OFF THE MASK</u>

ADAM ABD EVE

ABRAHAM AND SARAH

JACOB AND ESAU

MOSES

DAVID AND BATHSHEBA

ELIJAH

JACOB

PETER

ANANIAS AND SAPPHIRA

CHRISTIANS

FAMILY MEMBERS

SUNDAY MORNING MASK

☻ ☻ ☻ ☻ ☻ ☻ ☻ ☻ ☻ ☻

TABLE OF CONTENTS

PREFACE
 CHAPTER 1
 THE MASK OF COVERING UP....................................5

CHAPTER 2
THE MASK OF LYING....................................23

CHAPTER 3
THE MASK OF DECEPTION....................................33

CHAPTER 4
THE MASK OF RUNNING AWAY....................................43

CHAPTER 5
THE MASK OF UNFAITHFULNESS....................................55

CHAPTER 6
THE MASK OF HIDING....................................65

CHAPTER 7
THE MASK OF SELF-PITY....................................73

CHAPTER 8
THE MASK OF DENIAL....................................83

😊 😊 😊 😊 😊 😊 😊 😊 😊 😊

CHAPTER 9
THE MASK OF PRETENSE.................................91

CHAPTER 10
DO CHRISTIANS WEAR MASK?............................97

CHAPTER 11
THE MASK OF FAMILY MEMBERS....................105

CHAPTER 12
THE PULPIT MASK.....................................111

CHAPTER 13
SOMETHING TO THINK ABOUT..........................117

OTHER THOUGHTS...................................120

TESTIMONIES OF WEARING MASK....................125

EPILOGUE...128

ADDENDUM..131

Be Yourself

PREFACE

On March 20th, 2014, the first day of spring, the day after my birthday, I was on the treadmill doing my morning exercise. I was in the process of completing my second book, and I was asking God's guidance as to what my next assignment would be; suddenly the thought came to me, **take off the mask; be yourself.**

From the beginning of time man has been wearing a mask, and pretending to be someone else instead of being himself, and taking off the mask. Kids pretend all the time, and at Halloween, this is the time they love to dress up and pretend to be a certain character. Where did this desire to hide from someone comes from? Does anyone get hurt if we hide behind our masks? What can we do that will allow us to take off our mask, and be content to be ourselves? These are some of the things that will be discussed in this book, **Take off the mask,** based on some of our Bible characters.

Are you wearing a mask? Does anyone know who you are? So often we live in fear, and constantly have this thought, what if people really knew what I was really like? So many of us struggle with stuff in our lives, and we hide behind our mask pretending that all is well, but it is time to take off the mask, keep the mask off, and be our-self.

I do not believe everybody wears a mask. I believe there are people who are genuine in the things they do, and they do not have to wear a mask and pretend to be somebody else. There is a saying, "what you see is what you get," and these people are the real thing. So if you are not wearing a mask to cover things up, be thankful to God for who you are, but if you are wearing a mask to cover things up, it is time to take it off, and be yourself.

Being transparent in today's society is not very easy, it appears everyone has something to hide, but this is not true, there are people out there who are true to what they believe, and are trusting God in what they do. In whatever you and I do or say, let us not forget that we cannot hide from God.

Derrick M. Thompson, Sr.

● ● ● ● ● ● ● ● ● ●

WHAT IS A MASK?

A mask is described as "a covering for all or part of the face, worn to conceal our identity." It is normally worn on the face, typically for protection, disguise, performance or entertainment. Masks have been used from ancient times for both practical and ceremonial purposes. Masks are usually worn on the face, "although they may be positioned for effect elsewhere on the wearer's body."

The word "mask" appeared in English in the 1530's. This word is of uncertain origin, but one German author claims the word "mask" is originally derived from the Spanish masque la cara (literally, "more than the face" or added face").

Across the world the use of masks in "rituals or ceremonies is a very ancient human practice," even though masks can also be worn for protection, sports, in hunting, in feasts or wars, or as ornamentation.

There are different types of functional masks, such as medical masks; protective masks; disguise masks; occupational masks; sport masks; fashion masks and so on.

Medical Masks, this includes the oxygen mask, which is a piece of medical equipment protecting the burn tissue from contact with other surface, and minimize the risk of infection.   The surgical mask is a piece of medical equipment that helps in protecting both the surgeon and patient from acquiring infection from each other.

Protective Masks, these are pieces of kit or equipment worn on the head and face to offer protection to the wearer. In Roman "gladiatorial tournaments," masks were

☻ ☻ ☻ ☻ ☻ ☻ ☻ ☻ ☻ ☻

sometimes used. The protective mask in sport will often have secondary function making the wearer appear "more impressive as a competitor."

<u>Disguise Masks,</u> these are sometimes used for avoiding recognition. The mask acts as a form of protection for the wearer who wishes to assume a task without being identified by others.

<u>Occupational Masks,</u> falling in this category is the beaked mask; filter mask, gas mask, oxygen mask, and the welding mask.

<u>Sports Masks;</u> falling in this category is the face mask used in American football, baseball catcher's mask, diving mask, fencing mask, goaltender mask, kendo mask and so on.

<u>Fashion Masks,</u> these are decorative masks, and maybe worn as part of a costume outside of ritual or ceremonial functions.

Are you wearing a "disguise mask"? Is there a reason for wearing it? If not, just take it off, and be yourself.

Source: Wikipedia, the free encyclopedia.

Be Yourself

Be Yourself

☻ ☻ ☻ ☻ ☻ ☻ ☻ ☻ ☻ ☻

KEEP THE MASK OFF, AND BE YOURSELF

Take Off The Mask

● ● ● ● ● ● ● ● ● ●

TAKE OFF THE MASK

AND

BE YOURSELF

☻ ☻ ☻ ☻ ☻ ☻ ☻ ☻ ☻ ☻

GENESIS 3: 6-11

And when the woman saw that the tree was good for food, and that it was pleasant to the eyes, and a tree to be desired to make one wise, she took of the fruit thereof, and did eat, and gave also unto her husband with her; and he did eat.

And the eyes of them both were opened, and they knew that they were naked; and they sewed fig leaves together, and made themselves aprons.

And they heard the voice of the Lord God walking in the garden in the cool of the day: and Adam and his wife hid themselves from the presence of the Lord God amongst the trees of the garden.

And the Lord God called unto Adam, and said unto him, Where art thou?

And he said, I heard thy voice in the garden, and I was afraid, because I was naked, and I hid myself.

And he said, Who told thee that thou wast naked? Hast thou eaten of the tree, whereof I commanded thee that thou shouldest not eat?"

◆◆◆◆◆◆◆◆◆◆◆

☻ ☻ ☻ ☻ ☻ ☻ ☻ ☻ ☻

CHAPTER 1

THE MASK OF COVERING UP

(ADAM AND EVE)

TAKE OFF THE MASK

Have you ever tried to cover up something you have done wrong? You had a strange idea that no one would find out. That might have been what Adam and Eve thought, but they were wrong, because hiding behind a mask; hiding behind fig leaves, cannot make you hide from God.

From the beginning of time, man has been wearing a mask, pretending to be someone else, rather than being himself. Starting in 1956 there was an "American television panel game show," called **To Tell the Truth.** It is said that this show was "one of five game shows in the United States to have aired at least one new episode in at least six consecutive decades."

In this show, a panel of four celebrities was featured, and the object was for them to correctly identify "a described contestant who has an unusual occupation or experience." The main character is accompanied by two impostors who pretend to be the main character. The panelist would question the three contestants, the main character was sworn to tell the truth, but the impostors were allowed to lie. After questioning the contestants, the panelists attempt to identify which of the three contestants is telling the truth, and is therefore the main character.

Normally when I go to visit my older son and his family, our grand-daughter Kori-Lynne would hurriedly go to her grand-mother, but it would take sometime before she comes over to see me. On this particular day, as I entered the house, Kori-Lynne walked towards me, she was smiling, and she said hello grandpa. I picked her up, and kissed her. This was somewhat unlike Kori-Lynne, and very shortly I realized Kori-Lynne had something in mind. I went to the den, and Kori-Lynne started to fix me a meal on her toy stove, and then said she was the mother and I was the baby. Kori-Lynne for approximately forty five minutes played the role of a mother, and I was her baby. During this period of time, I played the role of a baby, as best as I could. The time came when I had to go, and I informed Kori-Lynne that we would go back to our normal role, I would be grandpa- and she would be the grand-daughter, we had to take off our masks or change our role play, and be ourselves again.

Quite often in a role play, a person might like the part they were playing, and may continue playing the part by their actions, instead of taking off the mask, and be them self. Just supposed I had continued playing the role as baby, and my grand-daughter playing the role as mother, what a strange world that would be?

Adam and Eve lived in a perfect environment, in the "Garden of Eden," a place they called home. God blessed Adam and Eve and they were instructed to be fruitful, to multiply, and to replenish the earth. They were to have dominion; they were the ones in control over the fish of the sea, the fowl of the air, and every living thing that moves upon the face of the earth.

Man had everything he needed, he could do whatever he wanted to do except for one thing. In Genesis 2 verses

● ● ● ● ● ● ● ● ● ●

16 and 17, man was given a command by God, "And the Lord God commanded the man, saying, "Of every tree of the garden thou mayest freely eat: But of the tree of the knowledge of good and evil, thou shalt not eat of it: for in the day that thou eatest thereof thou shalt surely die." This appears to have been a simple command, but which was disobeyed and lead to the fall of man.

As humans, we were created to be in subjection to God, and to look to him for our direction. Adam was given a command by God, he should not eat from one specific tree, "the tree of the knowledge of good and evil," but man disobeyed God's command. How could man in a perfect environment, having dominion over everything, disobey God's command? In the "Garden of Eden," in that perfect environment that man lived, there "was the serpent that was more subtil than any beast of the field which the Lord God had made. And he said unto the woman, Yea, hath God said, Ye shall not eat of every tree of the garden?" The woman replied to the serpent, "We may eat of the fruit of the trees of the garden; But of the fruit of the tree which is in the midst of the garden, God hath said, Ye shall not eat of it, neither shall ye touch it, lest ye die." The woman corrected the serpent, she pointed out to the serpent what God had said, when the serpent tried to bring doubt to her mind.

God had given man a command, which he must have told his wife about, but here we find the serpent speaking to the woman, and one might wonder where the man was. In Genesis 3 the latter part of verse 6 says, "she took of the fruit thereof, and did eat, and gave also unto her husband with her; and he did eat." Here is something to think about. As a young child growing up in Jamaica, I was informed through the preached word, and in Sunday school that Adam was somewhere in the Garden when Eve gave the fruit to him; but here in the passage it says,

"and gave also unto her husband with her." The question is, was Adam with his wife when the serpent spoke to her, and if so, why would the serpent not have spoken to Adam? As a child I was convinced that Adam was in the garden away from his wife, but not too long ago, I was told that Adam was with his wife. I was a bit confused as to what I had learned over the years, and to what came to my attention as an adult.

When you are confused, it is always a good thing to check things out that might have caused the confusion. Is it possible that Adam was in the garden and not by Eve's side when she was tempted by the serpent? For example, just supposed you were at home with your wife, and at a different location, and someone called and ask for your wife, would you say she is not there or would you call out to her or go and get her? I have noticed that this passage in some versions or translations the "with her," is excluded. For example in the "New Century Version," it reads like this, "So she took some of its fruit and ate it. She also gave some of the fruit to her husband, and he ate it." There are some things we might never be sure about, but one thing that we are sure about is that Eve disobeyed God's command and was deceived by the serpent.

Here we find God's perfect creation deceived by the serpent. The serpent was the craftiest of all creatures, and knew how to be deceptive. The serpent brought doubt into Eve's mind. Did God really say that you should not eat of every tree of the garden? Do you really believe you are going to die if you eat fruit from this tree? The truth is, you are not really going to die, for God knows that if you eat the fruit from this tree, your eyes will be opened, and you will be like gods knowing good and evil. Eve was tricked, she fell for the crafty plan of the serpent, and she took the fruit and eats it, and gave some to her

❂ ❂ ❂ ❂ ❂ ❂ ❂ ❂ ❂ ❂

husband. After eating the fruit their eyes were opened, and it was then they realized that they were naked. In their nakedness, in their sinfulness, they tried to cover up themselves, by sewing fig leaves and making aprons.

God's perfect creation in Adam and Eve had disobeyed God's direct command, and they tried to hide behind a mask by using fig leaves as aprons. Adam and Eve might have thought they could hide from God. They might have thought they could cover themselves up. They might have thought that God would not find out. As they thought on these things, as they thought on what they had done, "they heard the voice of the Lord God walking in the garden in the cool of the day;" and they then tried to hide from God.

Before man had sinned, man used to have sweet fellowship with God. Man used to commune with God, man had a relationship with God, but because of disobedience, because of sin, man tried to hide from the presence of the Lord. Man put on a mask, and was hiding amongst the trees of the garden.

The Bible says, in the latter part of Numbers 32 verse 23, "and be sure your sin will find you out;" "and you can be sure that you will not escape the consequences of your sin;" "and be sure that your sin will not go unpunished." As man was hiding, God called out to man, "Where art thou?" God knew where Adam was, God knew what Adam had done, God was not calling for information as to the whereabouts of Adam, but I believe God was calling for an explanation. Adam, where are you? Adam, what have you done? Adam, why are you hiding from me?

Adam, God's perfect creation now knew what it was to be fearful and guilty. He knew what it was like to cover things up. He now knew what it was like to be ashamed. In fear, in guilt and in shame he tried to answer the Lord, **"I heard thy voice in the garden, and I was afraid,**

because I was naked: and I hid myself." Lord, I have put on a mask; I am not what I used to be, I have disobeyed your direct instruction, I have failed. By the way Adam, how do you know that you were naked? Who gave you that information? Did you eat of the tree that I told you not to eat? Man was caught in a trap; he did not know what to do. Lord, that woman you gave me, the one call Eve, the one you gave to be with me, she gave me the fruit from the tree, and I did eat.

Man was responsible for his wife; he was supposed to take care of his wife. He was supposed to protect her at all times under all conditions, but here we find man blaming his wife for his failure. God asked Eve what she had done, why was Adam blaming her, and she said the serpent was at fault, I was tricked by the serpent, the serpent placed doubt in my mind, and I did eat. The serpent had no one to blame, and God placed a curse on the serpent. The curse is recorded in Genesis 3 verses 14 and 15, **"Because thou hast done this, thou art cursed above all cattle, and above every beast of the field; upon thy belly shalt thou go, and dust shalt thou eat all the days of thy life; And I will put enmity between thee and the woman, and between thy seed and her seed; it shall bruise thy head, and thou shalt bruise his heel."**

God said to the woman, **"I will greatly multiply thy sorrow and thy conception; in sorrow thou shalt bring forth children; and thy desire shall be to thy husband, and he shall rule over thee."**

Adam had failed God, and he had to suffer the consequences of his disobedience. In Genesis 3 verses 17 through 19, God said to Adam, **"Because thou hast hearkened unto the voice of thy wife, and hast eaten of the tree, of which I commanded thee, saying, Thou shalt not eat of it: cursed is the**

ground for thy sake; in sorrow shalt thou eat of it all the days of thy life; Thorns also and thistles shall it bring forth to thee; and thou shalt eat the herb of the field; In the sweat of thy face shalt thou eat bread, till thou return unto the ground; for out of it wast thou taken: for dust thou art, and unto dust shalt thou return."

Adam and Eve had failed God, and they tried to cover it up by putting on a mask. They decided to pretend that everything was alright. They must have thought that God could not see behind a mask. They must have thought they could hide their disappointment and dissatisfaction behind a mask. They must have thought everything will work itself out. When we wear a mask, what exactly are we trying to accomplish? How long can we hide what is bothering us on the inside, by trying to pretend that all is well?

As we look at our lives, how many times have we felt disappointment and dissatisfaction, and those around us gives us the impression it is alright, just wear the mask? So what do we do? We put on the mask and pretend all is well, life is great, it could not be better, even though we are filled with dissatisfaction and disappointment. In wearing the mask, we are saying nobody really knows what is happening on the inside. We are saying to ourselves we can cover things up as long as we want to, nobody will know of our cover up, and so we will just wear the mask. We are living in constant fear and wondering, **"What if people really know what I was like?"** What if the real me show up at work? What if the real me show up at church? What if the real me show up in the grocery store? What would happen if the mask was taken off, and what would others be saying about me?

Adam and Eve were stuck behind the mask. They had no real solution to their problem, and how to remove the mask. The fig leaves were their covering, and they found safety among the trees. There are people today who are hiding behind a mask, and they feel safe in doing so than to worry what the outcome might be if the mask is removed. It is risky trying to remove the mask, the real you will show up, but the mask must be removed in order to be yourself. Adam was faced with the all important question, **"where art thou?"** Adam tried to play it safe instead of trying to remove the mask.

God wants us to take a risk and take off the mask as He asks the question, **"where art thou?"** God wants us to get out of our comfort zone, take off the mask as He asks the question, **"where art thou?"** God wants us to confess our faults to Him, take off the mask as He asks the question, **"where art thou?"** It is not easy to take off the mask; the things that are wrong about us are hidden behind the mask; we are being destroyed inwardly, and our relationship with others and with God is being hindered, and so God is asking the question, **where art thou?"** It is mask removing time, and God wants us to come clean before Him, and confess to Him, as He asks the question, **"Where art thou?"**

It is so very easy to blame others for our problems. It is so very easy to see the many faults in others. It is so very easy to point our finger at our brother and our sister as Adam did, but the question is very personal for each of us to answer, **where art thou?"** The Bible says in Luke 6:41, **"And why beholdest thou the mote that is in thy brother's eye, but perceivest not the beam that is in thine own eye?"** How is it possible to see that speck in thy brother's eye, and fail to realize the beam that is in thine own eye?

I used to say quite often that we see people and everything on the outside appears to be alright, but we never know what is going on inside. It is so very easy to

☺ ☺ ☺ ☺ ☺ ☺ ☺ ☺ ☺

cover things up with the mask, and pretend that everything is alright. Let us not forget that God sees behind the mask, and He knows exactly who we are.

I remember as a young man in Jamaica, my pastor spoke on the topic **"be yourself**." It is so very easy to keep the mask on and try to be somebody else, but God wants each of us to be our-self, and take off the mask. God wants each of us to get out of the pretending mode, and be our-self. In order to be our-self, we have to own up to our failures, take the mask off, and confess to God. The Bible says in 1 John 1: 9, **If we confess our sins, he is faithful and just to forgive us of our sins, and to cleanse us from all unrighteousness."**

Are you wearing a mask? Does anyone know who you really are? If you are wearing a mask, then the time has come to take it off, and be willing take a risk into the unknown with the thought that God alone knows about tomorrow, and that He will take care of you. There is no need to wear a mask anymore, just keep it off, and be yourself.

<u>Think On These Things</u>.

In my office at home before I relocated, I have these words written over my door, **"Death and life are in the power of the tongue...."**(Proverbs 18:21a). It is so very easy to destroy others by the things we say. Sometimes we might say things not realizing what we are saying, forgetting the power that lies in what we say. James writes in James 3: 8-11, **"But the tongue can no man tame; it is an unruly evil, full of deadly poison. Therewith bless we God, even the Father; and therewith curse we men, which are made after the similitude of God. Out of the same mouth proceedeth blessing and cursing. My brethren,**

these things ought not so to be. Doth a fountain send forth at the same place sweet water and bitter?"

As we take off the mask and endeavor to be our self, let us watch the tongue in the things we say remembering **"that death and life are in the power of the tongue...."**

All over the world, on the first day of the year, people make resolutions as to what they intend to accomplish for the New Year.

On January 1st, 2015, I wrote down six things, and placed in my home office of things I am going to do or continue to do in the year 2015. It is not always easy to share things that are personal to us, but if sharing is going to help someone then I believe it is alright to share. 1. Be the best I can in serving the Lord in every way possible.

2. Love and taking care of my family (wife, children, grand-children...) in every way possible.

3. Be faithful to the service of the Master, and be a witness for Him; and be at peace with all men. ("If it be possible, as much as lieth in you, live peaceable with all men." Romans 12: 18)

4. Completing of my third book as time permits.

5. Whatever I do, I want my doing to glorify God, and if God is glorified then all is well.

6. Waiting patiently to hear from the Lord, "well done

☻ ☻ ☻ ☻ ☻ ☻ ☻ ☻ ☻ ☻

thou good and faithful servant..."

Note: All the time I have is now, and so I want to use my time wisely for the Lord, because tomorrow is not promised, it is in God's hands.

<u>Taking off the mask is not easy, but in order to be yourself, you have to take the risk and take the mask off.</u> You ask a friend, a love one, or possible a stranger, how are they doing, and even though they might be going through some testing time, they quite likely might answer that they are doing alright. It is hard to take the mask off and be yourself.

If things are alright, then it is alright to say you are alright; but if things are not alright, is it alright to say you are alright? No.

Depending on who is asking the question, maybe if things are not alright, you could say, it could be better; or just pray for me, or I am still holding on, or I am alive and grateful. Taking off the mask and being yourself is taking a risk, and not knowing what the result might be. The next time someone ask you, how are you doing, it may be best to think for awhile before answering.

On a certain Sunday morning I was on my way to church service, and on my way I said something that I thought was alright. As the church service progress, the pastor made reference to things people might say, and he made reference to what I had said. It then dawned on me, that the mask had to be taken off, and I had to be myself. Wearing that mask can be painful, and quite often bring serious consequences. Adam and Eve learned the hard

way that it is far better to obey God than to obey a serpent.

<u>Questions and comments</u>.

Adam and Eve were God's perfect creation, living in a perfect environment, but they choose to disobey God.

What did it cost Adam and Eve when they disobeyed God?

....

....

What do you think it would be like if Adam and Eve did not disobey God?

....

....

....

Is it your desire to obey God under all circumstances?

....

Be Yourself

Take Off The Mask

THOMPSON'S WORD SEARCH

ON ADAM AND EVE

D	T	E	V	E	U	S	U	T	W
Q	N	O	T	I	U	R	F	R	O
S	F	T	L	M	O	R	E	E	M
I	E	H	E	D	E	N	G	E	A
R	L	R	F	O	O	D	V	W	N
M	E	H	P	Z	E	N	K	Y	Q
G	A	R	D	E	N	R	I	S	U
I	P	T	S	C	N	P	T	O	Z
Z	P	W	X	Y	O	T	F	P	B
F	L	E	F	A	E	L	G	I	F
N	E	N	O	S	P	M	O	H	T

APPLE; EDEN

EVE; FIGLEAF

TREE; THOMPSON

GARDEN; FOOD

SERPENT; WOMAN; FRUIT

Be Yourself

☺ ☺ ☺ ☺ ☺ ☺ ☺ ☺

<u>NOTES</u>

⚫ ⚫ ⚫ ⚫ ⚫ ⚫ ⚫ ⚫ ⚫ ⚫

GENESIS 12: 10 -13

And there was a famine in the land: and Abram went down into Egypt to sojourn there; for the famine was grievous in the land.

And it came to pass, when he was come near to enter into Egypt, that he said unto Sarai his wife, Behold now, I know that thou art a fair woman to look upon:

Therefore it shall come to pass, when the Egyptians shall see thee, that they shall say, This is his wife: and they will kill me, but they will save thee alive.

Say, I pray thee, thou art my sister: that it may be well with me for thy sake; and my soul shall live because of thee.

GENESIS 20: 1-7

And Abraham journeyed from thence toward the south country, and dwelled between Kadesh and Shur, and sojourned in Gerar.

And Abraham said of Sarah his wife, She is my sister: and Abimilech king of Gerar sent and took Sarah.

But God came to Abimelech in a dream by night, and said to him, Behold, thou art but a dead man, form the woman which thou hast taken; for she is a man's wife.

But Abimelech had not come near her: and he said, Lord,

☻ ☻ ☻ ☻ ☻ ☻ ☻ ☻ ☻ ☻

wilt thou slay also a righteous nation?

Said he not unto me, She is my sister? and she, even she herself said, He is my brother: in the integrity of my heart and innocency of my hands have I done this.

And God said unto him in a dream, Yea, I know that thou didst this in the integrity of thy heart; for I also withheld thee from sinning against me: therefore suffered I thee not to touch her.

Now therefore restore the man his wife; for he is a prophet, and he shall pray for thee, and thou shalt live: and if thou restore her not, know that thou shalt surely die, thou and all that are thine.

◆◆◆◆◆◆◆◆◆◆◆◆◆◆◆◆◆◆◆◆◆◆

ABRAHAM AND SARAH

TAKE OFF THE MASK

⦿ ⦿ ⦿ ⦿ ⦿ ⦿ ⦿ ⦿ ⦿ ⦿

CHAPTER 2

THE MASK OF LYING (ABRAHAM AND SARAH)
ABRAM AND SARAI
TAKE OFF THE MASK

Have you ever tried to lie yourself out of a given situation? You know what you were doing was wrong, but in your mind you were saying, God will forgive, he will understand, and so you lied. Abraham and Sarah lied, they did not have to lie, but they did, and God did not like what they did.

Abraham was a man of faith. He was a friend of God, who had lived very close to God; and endeavored to please God in everyway. He was called by God to leave his country, his kindred, his father's house, and go to a land that God would show him. In Genesis 12: 1-3 we read these words, "Now the Lord had said unto Abram, Get thee out of thy country, and from thy kindred, and from thy father's house, and unto a land that I will shew thee: And I will make of thee a great nation, and I will bless thee, and make thy name great; and thou shalt be a blessing: And I will bless them that bless thee, and curse him that curseth thee: and in thee shall all families be blessed."

What would you do if you were told by God to get up and go; but you were not told where you were going? As you think about that question, Abram the friend of God simple obeyed the voice of God, to leave his country, leave his people, and leave his father's house. Abram trust was in God, and he knew everything was going to be alright. Who in their right mind would leave their homeland and do not know where they are going? If there is no doubt in your mind that God has spoken to you, then it is wisdom to obey the voice of God.

This great man of faith, a friend of God, left home with Sarai his wife, and other relatives in obedience to the voice of God. It is a wonderful thing when you know that you are obeying God, and that you are in God's will. It is a wonderful thing to know that your trust is in God, and that there is no doubt in your mind that God will take care of you. It is a wonderful thing to know that whether you are enjoying the good times or you are having your testing times, you can still rely on God. Abram's trust was in God, Abram was relying on God, but as he journeyed along, he hit some hard times, "there was a famine in the land."

Sometimes in the Christian walk we are going to meet up with some hard times. Sometimes in the Christian walk our faith will be tested. Sometimes in the Christian walk we might decide to make our own decisions, and forget to rely on God. Sometimes in the Christian walk we might try to take a detour to find an easier way out. Those so called easier way out might be dangerous in our Christian walk. Many of God's faithful servants have failed along the way because they tried to find an easier way out. Yes, there is "famine in the land," but God knows how to take care of His children in the midst of a famine. We should not try to escape the famine by ourselves, but we should depend on God, knowing that He will be faithful.

The Bible does not say that Abram asked God's permission to go to Egypt, but it does say, "and Abram went down into Egypt to sojourn there; for the famine was grievous in the land." It seems Abram was finding an easy way out. Here we find God's man, a friend of God, leaving Canaan to go to Egypt because there was a famine in the land.

Most of us as Christians do not like to hear about famines; we do not want to talk about famines; we do not want to read or see anything about famines, we want to enjoy the life of prosperity. As Abram and his wife came near to Egypt, this man of faith, this man who was a friend of God became fearful of his life, and his faith dwindled. Abram came up with a deceptive plan, a master plan, he decided to put on a mask and be somebody else. In order for his plan to work he made his wife a part of his plan.

Sarai was sixty-five years old at the time, she was a woman of beauty, and Abram, a friend of God and a man of faith, feared for his life. Abram came up with the idea that when the Egyptians should ask about her, she should say she was his sister. Abram came up with a plan of saying what we call today, "a little white lie," or "a half truth." It is true that Sarai was Abram's sister, but his half sister; and it was also true that Sarai was his wife. There is a saying, "oh what tangled web we weave, when we start to deceive." Sarai went along with Abram's plan, which worked for awhile. Pharaoh the king of Egypt treated Abram very kindly because of Sarai, as long as he was wearing a mask, as long as his deceptive plan was not revealed. The Bible says in Numbers 32: 23, **"and be sure your sin will find you out. The Bible also says in Proverbs 28: 13, "He that covereth his sins shall not prosper:"**

We serve a great and mighty God, a God who loves and forgives. God still loves us even when we sin. Abram had failed God, Abram was walking around wearing a mask, not only was he wearing a mask, but his wife was

☻ ☻ ☻ ☻ ☻ ☻ ☻ ☻ ☻ ☻

wearing a mask. Abram was pretending that all was well. Sometimes as Christians, it seems that we forget that we cannot hide from God; it seems that we forget that God knows all about us, it seems that we forget that a mask will not make us to be somebody else in the sight of God. The Bible says in psalm 139: 7 -10, **"Whither shall I go from thy spirit? or whither shall I flee from thy presence? If I ascend up into heaven, thou art there: if I make my bed in hell, behold, thou art there. If I take the wings of the morning, and dwell in the uttermost parts of the sea; Even there shall thy hand lead me, and thy right hand shall hold me."**

Abram God's man moved out of fellowship, and tried to protect himself by telling a lie. It seems Abram was just thinking about how to preserve himself. God had made a promise to Abram in Genesis 12:7, "Unto thy seed will I give this land:" Abram builded an altar to the Lord who appeared to him. Abram was having sweet fellowship with the Lord, but as he journeyed toward the south, he faced a problem, there was a famine in the land, and famines will cause us to do strange things.

Abram lied, and as a result he put his wife in great danger and his marriage at risk. Abram had failed God, but God still cared about him. It is wonderful to know that even in our failures, God still cares about us. God sent a warning to Pharaoh's house, and in Genesis 12: 17 we read, "And the Lord plagued Pharaoh and his house with great plagues because of Sarai Abram's wife." Pharaoh was in trouble because he believed the lie Abram had told him. Pharaoh called Abram and asked him three questions, "What is this that thou hast done unto me? Why didst thou not tell me she was thy wife? Why saidst thou, She is my sister?" The Bible did not say Abram gave an answer to the questions, but the mask of

☺ ☺ ☺ ☺ ☺ ☺ ☺ ☺ ☺

pretense was removed, and Pharaoh commanded that Abram be sent away along with his wife, and all that he had.

The question we might ask our self is did Abram learn his lesson? Did he learn how to keep the mask off, or did he forget? If as Christians when we are tested and tried, if we did not learn from our experience, God will allow us to go through a similar experience again. It is like a child who has failed to pass the current grade, and so have to repeat the grade.

It is amazing that Abraham the man of faith, and the friend of God, had planned with his wife Sarah that wherever they went she should say that he was her brother. In Genesis 20: 13 we read, "And it came to pass, when God caused me to wander from my father's house, that I said unto her, This is thy kindness which thou shalt shew unto me: at every place whither we shall come, say of me, He is my brother." This was Abraham's confession to Abimelech when Abraham was found out to be wearing the mask of lying.

Abraham had it all figured out that when trouble knocked on his door, he and his wife Sarah would put on their mask. What do you do when trouble knocks on your door? Do you tell the truth or do you put on that mask of lying? Do you try to cover things up, and try to tell yourself nobody will know about my cover-up? Do you tell yourself nobody knows me here, so it is alright to mask up? Abraham is in a country of strangers, a place called Gerar, and he boldly declares, she is my sister. When Abraham told that half lie the first time, or that little white lie, Sarah was in her sixties, but now Sarah is in her nineties, and still beautiful One may ask, how could a woman in her nineties be still beautiful? To be beautiful she had to be wrinkle free, not walking with a limp, but still being desirable in the eyes of man.

☻ ☻ ☻ ☻ ☻ ☻ ☻ ☻ ☻ ☻

Abraham had to protect himself, he had to put on that mask of lying by saying Sarah was his sister. As a result of this pretense, as a result of putting on this mask, his wife was in great danger. As Christian men, we are supposed to protect our wives from all danger, but how far are we supposed to go? Should we take matters into our own hands, or should we put it into the hands of God who is our great protector? Abraham a man of faith, a friend of God once again had failed God, he had sinned, and he had put on a mask.

When the king heard that Sarah was Abraham's sister, he sent and took her. King Abimelech no doubt had evil intentions, but God came to him in a dream. God informed him he would be a dead man, for the woman he had taken was a man's wife. Abimelech plead his case, and that he could not know what he was doing because he was deceived, and he was innocent of wrongdoing. He had believed a lie, and was on the verge of falling into sin, but God intervened.

Abimelech was told by God to "restore the man his wife; for he is a prophet, and he shall pray for thee, and thou shalt live: and if thou restore her not, know thou that thou shalt surely die, thou, and all that are thine." Abimelech was given a choice; he could obey the voice of God or suffer the consequence. Abimelech obeyed the voice of God, but he had a question for Abraham, "What sawest thou, that thou hast done this thing? Abraham had an answer, "Because I thought, Surely the fear of God is not in this place; and they will slay me for my wife's sake." It was time, Abraham had to take the mask off; it was time to stop pretending, and it was time for him to be himself, a man of faith, and a friend of God.

The old nature that we all possess is unable to fulfill God's intention for our lives. Sometimes that old nature will put on a mask, and be capable of fooling many

😊 😊 😊 😊 😊 😊 😊 😊 😊 😊

people. The old nature, the flesh, can never please God. When we accept Christ as Lord of our lives, we will have to let the old self stop looking good, because we are new creatures in Christ. The Bible says in 2 Corinthians 5: 17, "Therefore if any man be in Christ, he is a new creature: old things are passed away; behold, all things are become new." As Christians, as followers of Christ we should not resort to our old lifestyle because the old man is dead, crucified with Christ. The Bible says in Romans 6: 6, "Knowing this, that our old man is crucified with him, that the body of sin might be destroyed, that henceforth we should not serve sin."

When the old man is crucified, we now have a new walk, we now have a new talk, there is no more pretense, no more mask wearing because our aim is to be more, and more like Christ. Abraham the man of faith, the friend of God had failed God, but God extended his mercy to Abraham. Abraham had put his wife at risk by not telling the whole truth, but God extended his mercy to him. It is wonderful to know that even in our failures, God is still merciful. Sarah was restored to Abraham, and he was given presents. In Genesis 20: 14 we read, "And Abimelech took sheep, and oxen, and men servants, and women servants, and gave them unto Abraham, and restored him Sarah his wife." God does things we cannot understand; we cannot figure God out, so it is always best to take off the mask and be yourself.

Questions and Comments

Abraham was a man of faith, and a friend of God, why did he have to lie?

....

....

Take Off The Mask

Abraham placed his wife at great risk by putting on a mask; what would you have done if caught in a similar situation?

....

....

....

God showed mercy to Abraham despite what he had done; in what ways has God shown his mercy to you?

....

....

It is so quick to judge, and point the finger at someone else, but let us all remember, we are all here because of the mercy of God; we did not deserve it, and so all we can say is thank you Lord, and truly your mercy endures forever.

GENESIS 27: 19-24

And Jacob said unto his father, I am Esau thy firstborn; I have done according as thou badest me: arise, I pray thee, sit and eat of my venison, that thy soul may bless me.

And Isaac said unto his son, How is it that thou hast found it so quickly, my son? And he said, Because the Lord thy God brought it to me.

And Isaac said unto Jacob, Come near, I pray thee, that I may feel thee, my son, whether thou be my very son Esau or not.

And Jacob went near unto Isaac his father; and he felt him, and said, The voice is Jacob's voice, but the hands are the hands of Esau.

And he discerned him not, because his hands were hairy, as his brother Esau hands: so he blessed him.

And he said, Art thou my very son Esau? And he said, I am.

JACOB AND ESAU

TAKE OFF THE MASK

❀ ❀ ❀ ❀ ❀ ❀ ❀ ❀ ❀ ❀

CHAPTER 3

THE MASK OF DECEPTION (JACOB AND ESAU) TAKE OFF THE MASK

Have you ever tried to trick anyone? You had it all planned out, they quite likely will never know what you have done because you are wearing a mask, and they might not be able to see. You might be right, they may never find out, but God knows. Such was the case with Jacob, as he carried out his deceptive plan to his father Isaac.

The story of Jacob and Esau was one about relationship. As we read Genesis 27: 1-4, we find Isaac making a deathbed request to his older son Esau. **"And it came to pass, that when Isaac was old, and his eyes were dim, so that he could not see, he called Esau his eldest son: said unto him, My son: and he said unto him, behold here I am.**
And he said, Behold now, I am old, I know not the day of my death: Now therefore take, I pray thee, thy weapons, thy quiver and thy bow, and go out to the field, and take me some venison; And make me savoury meat, much as I love, and bring it to me, that I may eat; and that my soul may bless thee before I die."

Isaac did not know the day of his death, but now that he was old, he believed it was a good time to make the request to his older son Esau. In verses 5-10, we find out that Rebekah was listening when Isaac spoke to their son

Esau, and she advises their son Jacob to deceive his father Isaac. Here is what Rebekah said to Jacob, "Behold, I heard thy father speak unto Isaac thy brother saying, "Bring me venison, and make me savoury meat, that I may eat, and bless thee before the Lord before my death." This is what your father have said to your brother Esau, and this is what I am saying to you, **"Now therefore, my son, obey my voice according to that which I command thee. Go now to the flock, and fetch me from thence two good kids of the goats; and I will make them savoury meat for thy father, such as he loveth: And thou shalt bring it to thy father, that he may eat, and that he may bless thee before his death."**

In Genesis 25: 23, God made a promise to Rebekah, **"Two nations are in thy womb, and two manner of people shall be separated from thy bowels; and the one people shall be stronger than the other people; and the elder shall serve the younger."** God had made a promise, and Rebekah was hastening God's promise, instead of patiently waiting on God. This was the same problem Abraham and Sarah had, God had made them a promise, but they thought they were too old for the promise to be fulfilled, and tried to find another way for the fulfillment of the promise. So often as Christians we do not want to wait on God, but prefer to take matters into our own hands, forgetting that God knows what is best.

Jacob listened to his mother's plan, but there was a problem, and in verse 11 he related the problem to his mother, "Behold, Esau my brother is a hairy man, and I am a smooth man:" Mothers know how to fix things, and it is quite possible she might have said, "Is that all you are worried about?" Her exact words were, "Upon me be the curse, my son: only obey my voice, and go fetch me

☻ ☻ ☻ ☻ ☻ ☻ ☻ ☻ ☻ ☻

them." Jacob did what he was supposed to do, and Rebekah did what she had planned to do. Rebekah took matters into her own hands because she had a plan. So often we call Jacob by different names, and somehow forget who was behind all that deception. Rebekah prepared the "savoury meat" for Isaac, and then in her craftiness she prepared Jacob to be disguised as Esau.

Rebekah allowed Jacob to steal his brother's identity, and in verses 15-17 we read, **"And Rebekah took goodly raiment of her eldest son Esau, which were with her in the house, and put them upon Jacob her younger son: And she put the skins of the kids of the goats upon his hands, and upon the smooth of his neck: And she gave the savoury meat and the bread, which she had prepared, into the hand of her son Jacob."**

Jacob was now ready, the food was prepared, his identity was changed, and he put on his mask of deception. Jacob's father was blind, but he could still hear. In verse 18 we find Jacob saying to his father, "My father," Isaac must have been confused, and he said, "Here am I; who art thou, my son?" In verse 19 Jacob started to lie; he started to deceive his father, the mask of deception was on, "I am Esau thy firstborn." That was a lie, he was Jacob the second born. "I have done according as thou badest me." That was a lie; he did what his mother had told him to do. Isaac still could not understand what was happening, and asked Jacob, how he got things done so quickly, and Jacob said, "Because the Lord thy God brought it to me." Jacob did not hesitate to bring the Lord into the picture. When the mask is on, it is hard to see things the way they really are.

Have you ever found yourself in a bind, and try to use the Lord as your means of escape? Isaac was a man of God, and surely he knew that God would provide. He

☻ ☻ ☻ ☻ ☻ ☻ ☻ ☻ ☻ ☻

must have remembered when his father Abraham was about to offer him as a sacrifice, and how God made a way and provided a lamb. Even though Isaac must have remembered how God had provided, he still was not convinced. He might have said to himself, I am blind, but I am no fool. He then asked Jacob who was wearing the mask of deception, to come near so he could feel him to determine if he was his son Esau or not. Isaac was in doubt, and he wanted to know the truth. After feeling Jacob he said, "The voice is Jacob's voice, but the hands are the hands of Esau." Was Isaac convinced that he was speaking to Esau? Did he still have doubts? After he had blessed Jacob who he thought was Esau, he said, "Art thou my very son Esau?" and Jacob said, "I am."

After Jacob had lied again saying that he was Esau, Isaac asked for the venison so that he could eat. Isaac ate the venison, he drank wine, he kissed Jacob who he thought was Esau, and again he blessed him. A portion of the blessing was for people to serve him, and for nations to bow down to him. Jacob received his blessing by deception. He might have thought it was alright, and he tried to justify any lie or sin he committed since he knew God wanted him to have the birthright.

Jacob received his blessing, but soon after he received the blessing Esau discovered his deception. The Bible says in Numbers 32: 23, "But if ye will not do so, behold, you have sinned against the Lord: and be sure your sin will find you out." In Genesis 27: 30-38 Jacob's deception is discovered. As soon as Jacob, the deceiver received his blessing, and left his father's presence, his brother Esau "came in from his hunting." He had made savory meat at his father's request, and brought it to him. Esau had no idea what had just taken place, and he was now in for a great surprise. Do you like surprises? If the surprise is working in your favor then it might be alright, but if the

❀ ❀ ❀ ❀ ❀ ❀ ❀ ❀ ❀ ❀

surprise is working against you, then that's a different matter. I believe Esau was excited, he had followed his father's command, and now he was ready for his blessing. I wonder if there are people out there who are working as hard as they can, doing all the things that they are supposed to do, but are missing out on their blessing. Esau had sold his birthright to his brother, and he was headed in the wrong direction.

Esau came to his father and said, "Let my father arise, and eat of his son's venison, that thy soul may bless me." Esau received the shock of his life by the reply his father gave him, "Who art thou?" In reply Esau said, "I am thy son, thy firstborn Esau." I am the one that you have given a command to take my weapon, my quiver, and my bow, and to go out in the field, to go out to the open country, to hunt some wild game for you. I am the one that you ask to prepare some tasty food, some venison, so that you might eat. Esau might have jokingly said, do you remember me daddy? I am that one, and I am back, and I have completed what you have asked me to do. Isaac started trembling, he was shocked, and then he inquired; if you are the person that I had asked to do all these things, then who is that person who came into me, who had brought me the game he had hunted, I ate it, and blessed him? When Esau heard his father's words, he realized what had taken place, and he began to cry.

There was deception in Isaac's household. Jacob had deceived his father Isaac, and his brother Esau. Jacob, along with his mother's guidelines had used trickery to deceive those around him. There is deception all around, and as Christians we have to be very careful, so that we will not be easily deceived. In desperation, Esau cried out to his father for a blessing.

Isaac came to the conclusion, and informed Esau that Jacob, "came with subtilty, and hath taken away thy

blessing." Esau started to plead with his father for a blessing. He asked his father if he had a blessing reserved for him, but was told by Isaac that Jacob was made his lord, and all his brethren were given to him for servants. Esau had given away his birthright, and lost out on his blessings. Jacob had put on the mask of deception, deceiving both his father, and his brother, and Esau lost out on his blessing. Do not interfere with the blessing God might have for you.

Questions and Comments:

It was in the plan of God that Jacob would receive the blessing from his father Isaac, but he deceptively received the blessing. Was this the right thing to do? or should Jacob have waited on God?

....

....

....

Jacob lied to his father Isaac that he was Esau; Isaac lied that his wife Rebekah was his sister; Abraham lied that Sarah was his sister ((half sister). Is there a time in life when lying is alright? God hates a lying tongue (Proverbs 6: 16-17)

....

....

....

Be Yourself

Esau sold his birthright to his brother Jacob, but he was still looking for a blessing from his father. Why?

....

....

....

☺ ☺ ☺ ☺ ☺ ☺ ☺ ☺ ☺ ☺

<u>NOTES</u>

• • • • • • • • • •

SCRIPTURE

EXODUS 1: 7; 15-19;
2: 1-3; 11-15.

MOSES

TAKE OFF THE MASK

❂ ❂ ❂ ❂ ❂ ❂ ❂ ❂ ❂ ❂

CHAPTER 4

MASK OF RUNNING AWAY
(MOSES)
TAKE OFF THE MASK

Have you ever done something terrible, and you thought no one had seen you or knew what you did? You might have thought you are home free, and it is back to business as usual. Moses the prince of Egypt had committed murder, and he thought no one had seen him, but the very next day he realized he was wrong, and so he had to put on a "mask" and start running.

The story of Moses is fascinating, and shows how God can use a man no matter who that person might be. The children of Israel which came to Egypt "were fruitful, and increased abundantly, and multiplied, and waxed exceeding mighty; and the land was filled with them." (Exodus 1:7) The king of Egypt saw how rapidly the Israelites were multiplying, and so taskmasters were set over them to afflict them with their burdens." A strange thing happened, "the more they afflicted them, the more they multiplied."

The king's plan was not working, and so he instructed the Hebrew midwives that if a boy was being born to the Hebrew women that boy should be killed, but if a daughter was being born, that daughter should be saved. The Hebrew midwives feared God, and did not obey the king's instructions, but saved "the men children alive." When the devil cannot have his way, he will stop at nothing, and he will try to carry out his destructive plan,

☻ ☻ ☻ ☻ ☻ ☻ ☻ ☻ ☻ ☻

but God always have an escape route for his children. Isaiah writes in Isaiah 54: 17: "No weapon that is formed against thee shall prosper."

The king of Egypt called the midwives, and asked why his command was not obeyed. They informed the king that "the Hebrew women are not as the Egyptian women; for they are lively, and are delivered ere the midwives come in unto them."

Pharaoh charged all his people saying, "Every son that is born ye shall cast into the river, and every daughter ye shall save alive." Pharaoh's plan was to limit the rapid increase of the Israelites, by killing the newborn boy babies. Pharaoh had a plan, and God also had a plan.

A boy baby was born to a man of the house of Levi, who had married a Levite woman. The mother saw that the child was a "fine child," and after hiding him three months, she realized she could do this no longer. She prepared "an ark of bulrushes, and daubed it with slime and with pitch, and put the child therein; and she laid it in the flags of the river's brink." Pharaoh's daughter came down by the river for a bath, and as her maidens walked along the riverside, Pharaoh's daughter saw the basket among the reeds, and she sent her maid to get it.

God works in ways we cannot understand. He works in mysterious ways in order to carry out His plans. Miriam the sister of the baby who was in the basket, was right there, and she asked Pharaoh's daughter if she could get one of the Hebrew women to nurse the baby for her, and she agreed. Miriam got the baby's mother, and the mother was given the baby to nurse, and she was paid to do so. This baby who was supposed to die by the hands of Pharaoh, was found at the riverside by Pharaoh's daughter; the baby was given to the baby's mother to be cared for, and she was paid for her services. One would say at this point, we serve a great God.

Be Yourself

● ● ● ● ● ● ● ● ● ●

This child grew, and when he was older, he was taken to Pharaoh's daughter, and he became her son. The young boy was named Moses by Pharaoh's daughter, because he was drawn out of the water.

Moses was now a young man, and one day he went out to look at the condition of his brethren. Moses grew up in Pharaoh's house, he was like a prince, but he had not lost his identity, he was a Hebrew. As he viewed the condition of his people, he saw an Egyptian hitting a Hebrew. Moses looked around, and when he thought he was in the clear, he killed the Egyptian, and hid his body in the sand. Have you ever done something wrong, and thought that no one saw you, only to find out later that you were wrong? The story is told of a young boy who came across an apple tree, he knew he was wrong to pick an apple without asking, but he looked to his right, and looked to his left, and he saw no one, he was about to pick the apple when he heard a voice saying "you forgot to look up." Sometimes in our mind we might think nobody is seeing what we do, but we are wrong, because God sees everything we do.

Moses might have thought he was in the clear, he might have thought what he did was the right thing to do, but the following day he was in for a big surprise. As he walked around checking on the condition of his brethren, he saw two Hebrew men fighting. Moses the murderer, now became Moses the peacemaker, and he asked the one who was in the wrong, "Why are you fighting your brother?" Moses asked a very simple question which deserved a very simple answer. The answer Moses received was a shocker, and this answer turned his life around. Listen to the answer, "Who make thee a prince and a judge over us?" "Who appointed thee to be a master?" They might have been thinking, yes you are from king's house; yes you are a prince, but who gave

☻ ☻ ☻ ☻ ☻ ☻ ☻ ☻ ☻ ☻

you the authority to be our master? That was not the end of the conversation, there was more, "intendest thou to kill me, as thou killest the Egyptian?" "Do you mean to murder me as you murdered the Egyptian?"

News gets around, and Moses became fearful. The king heard what had taken place, and sought to kill Moses. What was Moses going to do? Could he ask Pharaoh for his forgiveness? Could he ask his friends in king's house to put in a good word for him? Could he ask the one who had become his mother to speak on his behalf? It is quite possible Moses could have done something, but in his mind the safest thing to do was to run. Moses put on his mask, took off his princely way of thinking, and went on the run.

It must be a hard thing to be on the run? Moses the prince was now a murderer, and a fugitive, and he was on the run. He might have thought that he could get away with murder, but his sinful action was exposed by one of his fellow brethren, and so he was on the run. Prince Moses was a wanted man, he was on the run and he ended up in the land of Midian. When you are on the run, the idea is to get away as far as possible from where you are. The idea is to blend in with those around, forget about who you really are, and take on a new lifestyle. In taking on a new lifestyle, he married into a Midianite family, quite likely with the intention of blending in, and thus being able to wear his "mask of running away."

For forty years, Moses successfully wore a mask of hiding from the Egyptian authorities. For forty years, Moses quite likely might have been hiding in fear wondering if one day he would be caught.

Forty years is a long time to be on the run. Forty years is a long time to be wearing a mask. Forty years is a long time to be away from your friends and family. It was at this time in Moses life when it seems life was over

☻ ☻ ☻ ☻ ☻ ☻ ☻ ☻ ☻ ☻

for him, because he was old, that he had an encounter with God. Maybe you are up in age; and maybe you are saying there is nothing else for me to do; maybe you are saying the best part of my life is in the past, think for awhile, maybe, the best is yet to come. What can you accomplish when you are eighty years old? If God is leading, you can say the best is yet to come. As time passed by the king Egypt died and the children of Israel cried out to God because they were under bondage, and God heard their groaning, and remembered the covenant with Abraham, Isaac and Jacob.

In Exodus 3 is recorded the turning point in Moses life, he had an encounter with God. When anyone has an encounter with God, they will not be the same anymore. As Moses was taking care of his father in law's flock, he came to Mt. Horeb, and the angel of the Lord appeared to him. Moses saw a bush burning, but the bush was not consumed. God has a way of getting our attention. Moses was curious and went to see what was happening. God saw what Moses was doing, and God called out to him, and told Moses to come near, and take off his shoes for he was standing on holy ground. Moses the former prince, the murderer, the fugitive, who was on the run for forty years, was now standing before God on holy ground. When you come into the presence of God you have to take off the mask. When you come into the presence of God you have to be yourself. When you come into the presence of God you have to listen to what God has to say. God told Moses who He was, and gave Moses special instructions. In Exodus 3:10 we read, **"Come now therefore, and I will send thee unto Pharaoh, that thou mayest bring forth my people the children of Israel out of Egypt."** Moses listened to what God had to say. Moses knew what kind of person he was. He knew he was the man who was wearing a mask, and so he asked

☻ ☻ ☻ ☻ ☻ ☻ ☻ ☻ ☻ ☻

the question in Exodus 3:11, **"Who am I, that I should go unto Pharaoh, and that I should bring forth the children of Israel out of Egypt?"**

Let me pause for a minute; this is no coincidence. I was in the midst of writing my book, when I heard a message being preached from one of our Camp Meetings. The speaker asked the question, "What is it in thy hand? Let it go." The message blessed me so much that I had to take the time to mention it on Facebook. Moses was asked the question in his encounter with God, "What is that in thine hand?" The question was asked not as if God was ignorant as to what it was, but to lead on to what He further had to say. The question God asked Moses is asked of us today. In order to be used by God, we have to let go what is in our hand, and allow God to use us. All Moses had in his hand was a rod, which represented all that he possessed, and he had to let it go in order to be used by God.

Moses the former prince; Moses the murderer; Moses the shepherd who was running away, hiding behind a mask, had an encounter with God, and he had to let go of that which was so important to him, his rod, which represented his livelihood. Moses was given a command by God to go back to Egypt, and to tell Pharaoh to let His people go.

For forty years Moses was wearing a mask; the Pharaoh that Moses knew was dead; and Moses had doubt in his mind that they would not believe him that he was sent by God. In Exodus 4 God had to prove Himself to Moses as to who He really was, and gave Moses three signs to present to Pharaoh. For the first sign Moses was told to cast his rod on the ground, and it became a serpent. He was then told to take the serpent by the tail, and it became a rod in his hand. For the second sign God told Moses to put his hand in his bosom, and when he did

❋ ❋ ❋ ❋ ❋ ❋ ❋ ❋ ❋ ❋

so and took it out, his hand was leprous as snow. God then instructed Moses to put his hand into his bosom again, and when he did so, and took it out of his bosom, his hand was cleansed of leprosy. God said to Moses, if they did not believe the first two signs, there was a third sign in which he should take the water from the river, and pour it upon the dry land, and when this was done, the water poured upon the dry land would become blood. God had demonstrated to Moses what He was going to do, but Moses was not satisfied, and so he started to make excuses.

As Christians, so often we try to make excuses when God is about to do a great work in our lives. Quite often we try to talk about our inadequacies when God is about to do something spectacular. What kind of excuses do you make to God? Lord I am too young, or Lord I am too old. Lord I don't think I am ready for this task, or I am inexperienced, and the list could go on and on. Moses had seen what God could do, but here we find Moses making excuses to God. In Exodus 4:10 this is what Moses said to God, "O my Lord, I am not eloquent, neither heretofore, nor since thou hast spoken unto thy servant: but I am slow of speech, and of a slow tongue." Based on the reply God gave to Moses, one might believe that Moses had a speech impediment, and so God would have to send his brother Aaron as his spokesman. In Acts 7:22 Luke writes about Moses, "And Moses was learned in all wisdom of the Egyptians, and was mighty in words and in deeds." Moses was well learned, but was trying to make excuses to the great God who knows all things.

When you are wearing a mask, it is sometimes difficult to think clearly. When you are wearing a mask you might try to make excuses out of a given situation. God had heard enough from Moses, and in Exodus 4 and the first portion of verse 14 it says, "And the anger of the

Lord was kindled against Moses, and he said, Is not Aaron the Levite thy brother? I know that he can speak well."

The man who was the former prince of Egypt; the man who was a murderer; the man who was on the run for forty years, came into the presence of the Lord, and his life was not the same anymore. When we come into the presence of the Lord we have to take off the mask. When we come into the presence of the Lord we have to humble ourselves, and be obedient to the call God has upon our lives. Moses tried to make an excuse of his inability to carry out God's plan, but Moses had to bow to the will of God.

There is a saying, "you can run but you can't hide." Moses ran as far away as he could from Egypt. He thought he was safe in his new environment. He settled down with his new family, and might have though that all was well, but after 40 years things started to change, and Moses had to remove the mask and return to Egypt.

Questions and Comments:

Moses might have thought he was doing right by running away from Egypt to Midian and starting a new life. Do you think Moses was justified in what he did? How does the saying, "the end justifies the means," apply in this case?

....

....

....

....

Be Yourself

Why did Moses have to go to Midian?

....

....

God appeared unto Moses in a burning bush, what was so significant about the burning bush?

....

....

....

In what way has God revealed Himself to you, and did the revelation make a difference in your life?

....

....

NOTES

☻ ☻ ☻ ☻ ☻ ☻ ☻ ☻ ☻ ☻

SCRIPTURE
2 SAMUEL 11: 1-27

😊 😊 😊 😊 😊 😊 😊 😊 😊 😊

DAVID AND BATHSHEBA

TAKE OFF THE MASK

● ● ● ● ● ● ● ● ● ●

CHAPTER 5

THE MASK OF UNFAITHFULNESS (DAVID AND BATHSHEBA) TAKE OFF THE MASK

The Bible says in Proverbs 28:13 "He that coverereth his sin shall not prosper: but whoso confesseth and forsaketh them shall have mercy." David was considered as a man after God's own heart. In Acts 13:22 we read, "And when he had removed him, he raised unto them David to be their king; to whom also he gave testimony, and said, I have found David the son of Jesse, a man after mine own heart, which shall fulfil all my will."

The story of David and Bathsheba could be regarded by some as a story of judgment, and condemnation, and by others as a story of grace and restoration. The story shows to us how great men of God if not careful, can fall into sin. We have so many stories of great men of God who have fallen into moral failure because they have taken their eyes off the Lord.

David was supposed to be in battle, but the Bible says, "that David sent Joab, and his servants with him, and all Israel." The Bible says, "But David tarried still in Jerusalem." So often we get into trouble when we are at the wrong place at the wrong time. David was supposed to be in battle; but instead he was at home relaxing. While David was relaxing at home; while he was taking it easy instead of being on the battle-field; the Bible says in 2 Samuel 11:2, "And it came to pass in an eveningtide,

☻ ☻ ☻ ☻ ☻ ☻ ☻ ☻ ☻ ☻

that David arose from off his bed, and walked upon the roof of the king's house:" As David was walking upon the roof of his house he saw a beautiful woman bathing. What David saw was by accident, but he must have kept on looking; the Bible says in James 1:10, "Then when lust hath conceived, it bringeth forth sin: and sin, when it is finished, bringeth forth death."

David could have turned away, stop walking on the roof, and go back to bed. Turning away was not David's intent, but David was immediately attracted to her. David followed up with what he saw, and sent messengers to find out who she was.

David knew nothing about this woman next door, all he knew was that he saw a beautiful woman bathing. The messengers came back, and reported to David. David was told that this woman was Bathsheba, who was the daughter of Eliam, and wife of Uriah. Having been told that Bathsheba was married, this should be a red flag for David, but since he was king, he must have believed he could do anything. Somehow David must have had temporary amnesia, and had forgotten what the Bible said in Exodus 20: 14, "Thou shalt not commit adultery." There are many who are in high places doing things they should not be doing, and it is time to take off the mask and stop pretending.

Sometimes as Christians we might get caught up in the moment, realizing that something is wrong, but still go ahead and do it. Even though David knew Bathsheba was married; even though he knew that her husband was out on the battlefield fighting; even though he knew he could not hide from God, the Bible says in 2 Samuel 11: 4, "And David sent messengers, and took her; and she came in unto him, and he lay with her; for she was purified from her uncleanness: and she returned unto her house."

David must have thought he had a one night stand

● ● ● ● ● ● ● ● ● ●

with Bathsheba; he must have thought her husband would never find out, and if he does what would he do. He must have thought he had everything under control. Sometimes in life we might think we have everything under control. Sometimes we might think no one will ever find out what was done, but we forget that we cannot hide from God.

No one likes to receive bad news. After David had committed adultery; after he thought all was well, he received some bad news. In 2 Samuel 11: 5 we read, "And the woman conceived, and sent and told David, and said, I am with child." Bathsheba was pregnant, and the child she was carrying was not for her husband Uriah, but for David, "the man after God's own heart." What was David going to do? He had to find a way to cover things up, because it would not be easy walking around with a mask, pretending to be somebody else.

The great king David was nervous that his unfaithfulness and his sin of adultery would be found out. David came up with a plan, he called for Uriah to come home so that he could spend the night with his wife Bathsheba, and maybe this act would cover up David's sin of adultery. Uriah was instructed by David to go down to his house, to wash his feet, but Uriah refused to follow the king's instructions, to be with his wife while his fellow men were fighting. Uriah was a loyal soldier, but he felt the need of disobeying the king's command. David was not pleased, his deceptive plan had not worked, but he was not about to give up. David had gone too far, and he had to find other ways to get Uriah to go down to his house, but his plans failed.

Uriah was free to go back to battle, and David wrote a letter to Joab and sent it by the hand of Uriah. Uriah was carrying the death wish of David that was sent by him to Joab. In this letter, Joab was instructed to "Set ye Uriah

☻ ☻ ☻ ☻ ☻ ☻ ☻ ☻ ☻ ☻

in the forefront of the hottest battle, and retire ye from him, that he may be smitten, and die." Here was God's man; the one who was a man after God's own heart apparently forgetting who he really was and putting on the mark of unfaithfulness. (Ref. Acts 13:22)

As a Christian, have you ever forgotten who you really are? Have you ever put on that mask of unfaithfulness and be deceptive in what you do? Have you ever forgotten to allow your light to shine in a darkened world, or do you allow yourself to hide behind a mask?

Joab the loyal soldier, followed the instructions of his commanding officer David, with no questions asked. Apparently Joab might not have known what David did, but it was important for him to obey the king's command. Uriah had done nothing wrong; he was a faithful soldier, but his life was taken from him because David tried to cover up his sins, and pretended that all was well.

David continued with business as usual as if nothing was wrong. Uriah was dead, and he might have thought all would be well. What an awful thing for a child of God to be walking around and pretending all is well. Even though David was a man after God's own heart; even though in the past David had faithfully carried out God's plan for his life, God was displeased with David. The Bible says in 2 Samuel 11: 27, "But when the mourning was past, David sent and fetched her to his house, and she became his wife, and bare him a son. But the thing displeased the Lord."

David was walking around with the mask of unfaithfulness. He might have thought no one would find out, but forgot that God sees and knows all things, and that he could not hide from God. It is a dangerous thing to be pretending all is well. David knew that he served a merciful God. He knew that he served a God who is loving and forgiving, but he continue wearing the mask of unfaithfulness.

Thank God we have a God who is a forgiving God, and whose mercy endures forever. David said, "O give thanks unto the Lord: for he is good: for his mercy endureth forever." God always have someone to carry His word despite how things might appear to be. In 2 Samuel 12 God sent Nathan the prophet to speak to David by using a parable. After David had heard the parable, he was very angry, and said to Nathan in 2 Samuel 12: 5, "As the Lord liveth, the man that hath done this thing shall surely die." David had pronounced the sentence of death upon the man who had done wrong in the parable, and Nathan said to David, "thou art the man."

Is it possible David had forgotten what he had done? Is it possible he felt comfortable wearing the mask of unfaithfulness? Nathan reminded David what God had done for him, and how he had despised the commandment of the Lord, and had done evil in the sight of God. David had failed God, he was exposed for his unfaithfulness, and in 2 Samuel 12: 13 David confessed his sins, "And David said unto Nathan, I have sinned against the Lord." What a wonderful thing to know that God is a merciful God, and when we earnestly seek Him, He will hear and answer our prayer. David confessed, "And Nathan said unto David, The Lord also hath put away thy sin; thou shalt not die."

Despite David's failure; despite David wearing the mask of unfaithfulness; when David said, "I have sinned against the Lord," when he confessed his sin, God extended His mercy and forgave him. In Psalm 51 we find David's prayer of forgiveness. In this Psalm we find David crying out to God for mercy, "Have mercy upon me, O God....." Not only did he cry out for mercy, but he acknowledged his transgression. He realized he was wearing the mask of unfaithful**ss**. David realized the

☻ ☻ ☻ ☻ ☻ ☻ ☻ ☻ ☻ ☻

time had come to stop pretending, and come clean before God. David was willing to take off the mask, and be the person God wanted him to be.

Whenever we fail God, we have to come clean before God as we seek His forgiveness. David wanted a special cleansing from God that only God could give, and he wanted his joy to be restored. Hear these words from David in verses 7 and 8 coming from a sincere heart, "Purge me with hyssop, and I shall be clean: wash me, and I shall be whiter than snow. Make me to hear joy and gladness; that the bones which thou hast broken may rejoice." In verse 10 David says, "Create in me a clean heart O God: and renew a right spirit within me."

David the man who had failed God; David the man who had put on the mask of unfaithfulness; David the man who had strayed away from God, was now restored. To be restored is "to bring back to an original condition." Even though David had failed God, he has been looked upon as a man after God's own heart. So often when we hear the name king David, we often go back to him wearing the mask of unfaithfulness. When we hear the name king David we quite often go back to that one night stand he had with Bathsheba who later became his wife. Yes, David had failed God. Yes David had asked God for forgiveness, and God extended His mercy and forgave him. God forgives and forgets, and David is remembered today as the greatest king of Israel.

Are you wearing a mask? Do your friends know who you really are? David wore a mask, and he thought all was well until Nathan the prophet revealed to him where he stood. When David saw where he stood, he went to God and confessed his sins, God forgave him, and the mask was removed. Thank God, God still forgives and forgets.

☺ ☺ ☺ ☺ ☺ ☺ ☺ ☺ ☺ ☺

<u>Questions and Comments:</u>

David was supposed to be in battle, but he was at a place where he did not belong. What if David had been in the battle, and not on his roof walking around?

....

....

....

....

David love the Lord, but he failed the Lord. What can we do to avoid what happened to David from happening to us?

....

....

....

Does being a leader exempt us from doing what is right?

....

....

☺ ☺ ☺ ☺ ☺ ☺ ☺ ☺ ☺

62

<u>NOTES</u>

😊 😊 😊 😊 😊 😊 😊 😊

SCRIPTURE

1 KINGS 19: 1-8

ELIJAH

TAKE OFF THE MASK

❂ ❂ ❂ ❂ ❂ ❂ ❂ ❂ ❂ ❂

CHAPTER 6

THE MASK OF HIDING (ELIJAH) TAKE OFF THE MASK

In 1 Kings 19 is the story of the great prophet Elijah on the run, and he has put on the mask of hiding. In 1 Kings 18 Elijah had demonstrated to the prophets of Baal who the true God was. On Mount Carmel Elijah had called down fire from heaven that consumed his burnt sacrifice. On Mount Carmel the prophets of Baal were taken and were slain at the brook Kishon. On Mount Carmel Elijah had experienced the mighty hand of God, and now we see Elijah on the run, and he had put on the mask of hiding. Why was Elijah on the run? Why was Elijah hiding? There was a death threat out on the life of Elijah. Jezebel, the wife of king Ahab had taken matters into her own hands, and in 1 Kings 19 verse 2 Jezebel sent a message to Elijah saying, "So let the gods do to me, and more also, if I make not thy life as the life of one of them by tomorrow about this time."

When we receive bad news, it can bring about discouragement. When our lives are being threatened it might cause us to be on the run, and to go into hiding. God's man had experienced the supernatural power of God. The hand of the Lord was so mighty on Elijah that he ran before Ahab's chariot to Jezreel. This same man, God's prophet, found himself in a situation where he

☻ ☻ ☻ ☻ ☻ ☻ ☻ ☻ ☻ ☻

became scared, fearful, exhausted, depressed, and wanting to die. It seems Elijah was in a very bad shape. Have you ever found yourself in the house of God praising and rejoicing in God; like Elijah you might have found yourself on the mountain top, but shortly after something could happen that changed your mountain top experience. Wonderful things may take place on the mountain top, but it is in the valley that we are being tested.

In one of our recent Bible Class we talked about mountain top experiences, and the question was asked, do you need a breakthrough? Let me share with you a few things we talked about in that Bible Class. We said that, Peter, James and John had witnessed the glorious transfiguration of our Lord on the mountain. They had a mountain top experience. It was so great that Peter said, "Lord, it is good for us to be here. "Mountains often had a significant role in God's dealings with His people." It was on Mount Ararat that Noah's ark came to rest after the flood. It was on Mount Moriah, Abraham was asked to make a sacrifice of his son Isaac, and God provided the Ram as a substitute. It was on Mount Carmel Elijah challenged the false prophets of Baal to a contest to see which God would answer by fire, and God, Jehovah God, not Baal, answered by fire. Mountain top experiences are good, but it is in the valley that we are really tested.

Elijah on his run went a day's journey into the wilderness, and came and sat under a juniper tree, and he requested for himself that he would die, and said, "It is enough; now, O Lord, take away my life; for I am not better than my father." As Elijah "lay and slept under a juniper tree," an angel touched him and said, "Arise and eat." God has a way of giving us renewed strength when we are cast down. The psalmist asks the questions in psalm 42: 5, "Why art thou cast down, O my soul? and

☺ ☺ ☺ ☺ ☺ ☺ ☺ ☺ ☺ ☺

why art thou disquieted in me?" The psalmist goes on to give encouragement and hope in God, "hope thou in God: for I shall yet praise him for the help of his countenance." It seems Elijah had lost hope, and now he is on the run trying to hide from God with his mask on.

Have you ever felt hopeless, discouraged and do not know what to do? Have you ever felt that everyone has turned their backs on you? It is in those times of discouragement, in those times of hopelessness that God steps in. The angel told Elijah to arise and eat, and when he looked there was food prepared for him, "there was a cake baken on the coals, and a cruise of water at his head. "Elijah obeyed the angel, and he ate and drank, and laid down again.

The journey Elijah was going to be on would be a great journey, and so the angel came and touched Elijah a second time and told him to arise and eat. Elijah arose and ate and drank, and felt strong, and "walked 40 days and nights to Mount Horeb, the mountain of God." It is so good to know that God knows exactly what we need. Elijah in his exhausted condition was ready to die. Elijah in his hopelessness, saw no way of getting away from Jezebel, but had renewed strength after he was fed by the angel of God. When we feel that we are fainting, God gives us power. When we feel we have no might God gives us strength. In Isaiah 40: 29 we read, "He giveth power to the faint; and to them that have no might he increaseth strength."

With renewed strength Elijah came to a cave and stayed there. It was in the cave that the word of the Lord came to Elijah, and he was asked what he was doing there. This man of God who had put on the mask of hiding; this man of God who had requested to die was now in the very presence of God and had to give an answer to God. It seems Elijah was having a pity party as

❂ ❂ ❂ ❂ ❂ ❂ ❂ ❂ ❂ ❂

he answered the Lord. Elijah replied, "I have been very zealous for the Lord God of hosts: for the children of Israel have forsaken thy covenant, thrown down the altars, and slain thy prophets with the sword; and I, even I only am left; and they seek my life, to take it away." Elijah with the mask on could not see clearly, and he thought he was the only one left. In those times in life when we might think we are all alone, God is always there.

It is wonderful to know that we are not alone. It is wonderful to know that God is always there even though sometimes we might not think so. God instructed Elijah to "Go forth, and stand upon the mount before the Lord. And, behold, the Lord passed by and a great and strong wind rent the mountains, and brake in pieces the rocks before the Lord; but the Lord was not in the wind: and after the wind an earthquake; but the Lord was not in the earthquake: And after the earthquake a fire: but the Lord was not in the fire: and after the fire a still small voice."

Elijah had tried to answer the Lord when he was asked the question in verse 9, "What doest thou here, Elijah?" In verse 10 Elijah was having a pity party believing he was the only one left, and now they were seeking his life. After Elijah had gone through his pity party God gave Elijah some instructions as to what he should do; and then informed Elijah that he was not all alone as he might have thought. In verse 18 God reminded Elijah with these words, "Yet I have left me seven thousand in Israel, all the knees which have not bowed unto Baal, and every mouth which hath not kissed him." That was good news, Elijah was not alone, and there were seven thousand in Israel who had not bowed to Baal.

When we are wearing a mask it is difficult to think properly. When we are wearing a mask it is difficult to see clearly. When we are wearing a mask things are not the

way they are supposed to be, but when the mask is taken off an immediate change takes place. Now that the mask is taken off, Elijah was able to fulfill God's plan for his life. The prophet Elijah was no longer despondent; the prophet no longer had lost hope; the prophet no longer believed that death was the answer, but was now ready to fulfill God's plan for his life.

God has a plan for your life and my life. It is a wonderful plan, but it will not take place if we are hiding behind a mask. We have to remove the mask, and take heed to God's plan. In Jeremiah 29: 11-13 (NIV) we read, "For I know the plans I have for you, plans to prosper you and not to harm you, plans to give you hope and a future. Then you will call upon me and come and pray to me, and I will listen to you. You will seek me and find me when you seek me and find me when you seek me with all your heart."

Questions and Comments:

Elijah had seen the mighty manifestation of God's power on Mount Carmel when he called down fire from heaven that consumed his burnt sacrifice. Elijah had experienced the mighty hand of God, but now he is on the run. Why?

....

....

Elijah became despondent and wanted to die. What are some things that might cause despondency in our lives?

....

....

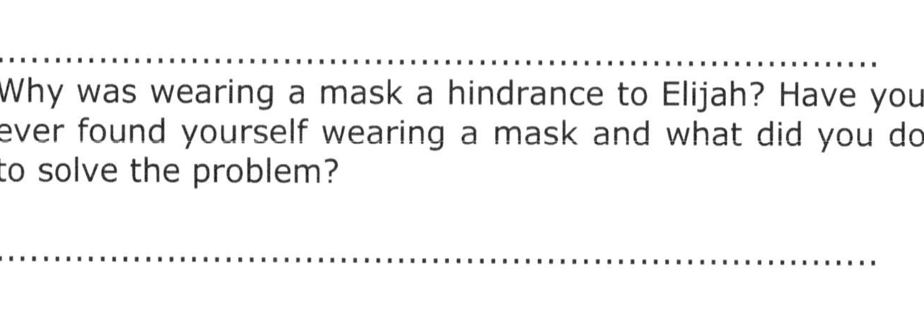

....

Why was wearing a mask a hindrance to Elijah? Have you ever found yourself wearing a mask and what did you do to solve the problem?

....

....

☻ ☻ ☻ ☻ ☻ ☻ ☻ ☻ ☻

SCRIPTURE
JONAH 1: 1-5; 1: 10-11 & 15; 4:1-3

😊 😊 😊 😊 😊 😊 😊 😊

JONAH

TAKE OFF THE MASK

❀ ❀ ❀ ❀ ❀ ❀ ❀ ❀

CHAPTER 7

THE MASK OF SELF-PITY
(JONAH)
TAKE OFF THE MASK

When God speaks to us and we know it is God's voice, it is always best to obey God's voice or suffer the consequences. In the book of Jonah it deals with a prophet of God called Jonah, who was given an assignment by God, but he chooses to disobey God's command. The assignment was a very simple one as recorded in Jonah 1: 2, "Arise, go to Nineveh, that great city, and cry against it; for their wickedness is come up before me." Why is it so easy to disobey God's voice? Why is it so very easy wanting to have things our way? All Jonah had to do was to get up and go to Nineveh and cry out against it. Jonah did not question his assignment, but the Bible says in Jonah 1: 3, "But Jonah rose up to flee unto Tarshish from the presence of the Lord, and went down to Joppa; and he found a ship going to Tarshish: and he paid the fare thereof, and went down into it, to go with them unto Tarshish from the presence of the Lord."

In trying to flee from the presence of God, he put on a mask, and it seems everything was working out for Jonah. He went to Joppa, and there he found a ship going to Tarshish. Have you ever found yourself doing something, that somehow you knew it was wrong, and you might even say to yourself God is working this out for my good. Jonah paid the fare and went on the ship going to Tarshish trying to flee from the presence of the Lord. Jonah the prophet should have known that he could not flee from the presence of the Lord. Jonah should have known that he could not hide from God. Jonah should have known that even in the bottom of the ship, away from all his friends, God was there. The Bible says in Psalm 139: 7-10, **"Whither shall I go from thy spirit? Or whither shall I flee from thy presence? If I ascend up into heaven, thou art there. If I take the wings of the morning, And dwell in the uttermost parts of the sea; Even there shall thy hand lead me, and thy right hand shall hold me."**

God the Almighty God got Jonah's attention by sending out a great wind into the sea. In Jonah 1:4 we read, " **"But the Lord sent out a great wind into the sea, and there was a mighty tempest in the sea, so that the ship was like to be broken."** There was turmoil on board the ship, because God's prophet chose to disobey the voice of God. When we disobey God's voice, when we attempt to run away from God, there will be problems. The mariners were afraid, and they all cried out to their gods, and cast things overboard to lighten the ship, but to no avail. Jonah was a masked man in the sides of the ship, and was sleeping during "the great wind." The shipmaster came to Jonah and asked why he was asleep, and asked him to call upon his God. When you are wearing a mask; when you are running away from God; when you have decided to disobey the voice of God, it would be difficult to call upon God.

The men in the ship were determined to find out what had caused the great wind, and so they decided to cast lots, and the lot fell on Jonah. It was determined that

Be Yourself

Jonah was the one responsible for the evil that was come upon them, and Jonah was confronted with several questions to answer. Jonah was finally asked what they should do that the sea might become calm, and he said, "Take me up, and cast me forth into the sea; so shall the sea be calm unto you: for I know that for my sake this great tempest is upon you." When we disobey God and try to do things our way, we will have to suffer the consequences of our disobedience. When we think we can go somewhere where no one will know who we are, God knows; and our sin will find us out. Casting Jonah overboard did not seem to be the answer to the problem, and they tried their very best to bring the ship to land, but it did not work.

Jonah was cast overboard, "and the sea ceased from her raging." Jonah the masked man had disobeyed God, but despite what Jonah had done, God still cared for him. God prepared a great fish to swallow Jonah, and the Bible says, "And Jonah was in the belly of the fish three days and three nights."

In the belly of the fish, Jonah had a prayer meeting. In the belly of the fish, Jonah cried out to God. In the belly of the fish, God heard Jonah's prayer. It is wonderful to know that no matter where we are, no matter what condition we might find ourselves in, when we sincerely cry out to God, He will hear our cry. As Jonah cried out to God, God heard his prayer, and the Bible says in Jonah 2: 10, "And the Lord spake unto the fish, and it vomited out Jonah upon the dry land."

What do you do when God gives you a second chance? What do you do when God extends His mercy to you? David writes in Psalm 42: 11 "Why art thou cast down, O my soul? and why art thou disquieted within me? Jonah had disobeyed God; he suffered the consequence of his disobedience but God extended His mercy. In Jonah 3: 1

& 2 we read these words, "And the word of the Lord came unto Jonah the second time saying. Arise, go unto Nineveh, that great city, and preach unto it the preaching that I bid thee."

The first time God spoke to Jonah, the Bible says in Jonah 1: 3' " But Jonah rose up to flee unto Tarshish from the presence of the Lord, and went down to Joppa; and he found a ship going to Tarshish: so he paid the fare thereof, and went down into it, to go with them unto Tarshish from the presence of the Lord." The second time God spoke to Jonah, he had prayed to God and now he had a new purpose, he was now a different man, a change had taken place. In Jonah 3: 3a we read these beautiful words, "So Jonah arose, and went into Nineveh, according to the word of the Lord."

So many times as Christians we find ourselves in trouble because we have disobeyed the voice of God. So many times we could avoid going through hardship if we had obeyed the voice of God. Sometimes what God might say to us might seem foolish, but as long as we know it is God speaking, all we have to do is obey. God told Abraham to leave his homeland not knowing where he was going, and all Abraham did was to get up and go because he knew God would take care.

Jonah went from the belly of the fish to the battlefield to declare the word of God. Jonah had what he could call "holy boldness," as he started to declare the word of God. The first time around Jonah "fled from the presence of the Lord," but now things have changed. Jonah had something he wanted to say, and now he was not afraid to declare God's word. In Jonah 3: 4 we read, "And Jonah began to enter into the city a day's journey, and he cried, and said, Yet forty days, and Nineveh shall be overthrown."

Jonah declared God's word, and the people of Nineveh

❀ ❀ ❀ ❀ ❀ ❀ ❀ ❀ ❀ ❀

believed God. They proclaimed a fast, "and put on sackcloth, from the greatest of them even to the least of them." The king was informed, laid aside his robe; he covered himself with sackcloth, and sat in ashes. What a wonderful thing had taken place; the people of Nineveh believed God, and trusted God would repent, "and turn away from his fierce anger." God saw the works of the Ninevites "that they had turned from their evil way, and God repented of the evil that he had said he would do unto them, and he did it not."

One would believe that Jonah would be happy that the people of Nineveh had repented from their evil ways. One would believe that Jonah would be rejoicing to see an entire nation turned to God. One would believe that Jonah would be praising God, but the bible says in Jonah 4:1, "But it displeased Jonah exceedingly, and he was angry." God's prophet was angry because God had showed His mercy to an entire nation. God's prophet was so angry so he put on the mask of self-pity. Jonah was so angry that he was willing to die. In Jonah 4:3 Jonah says, "Therefore now, O Lord, take, I beseech, my life from me, for it is better for me to die than to live." Jonah had just witnessed the mighty hand of God in the salvation of a nation, but here Jonah is showing displeasure of what God had done."

Have you ever felt sorry for yourself? Have you ever found yourself having a pity party? Have you ever found yourself upset with God because of what has happened? Normally we are not upset when we see others are being saved, but we rejoice in the Lord. For an entire nation to be saved that would be constant rejoicing and praise to God for what had taken place, but here the prophet Jonah was displeased for what God had done.

God saw Jonah having a pity party. God saw Jonah having on the mask of Self-Pity, and then asked Jonah,

☻ ☻ ☻ ☻ ☻ ☻ ☻ ☻ ☻ ☻

"Doest thou well to be angry?" When faced with the question from God, Jonah refused to answer, but went out of the city; made a booth, sat under it, and watched to see what would happen to the city. The people had turned to God; the people had sought God's forgiveness, but here we find Jonah waiting to see what would happen to the city.

God had to teach Jonah a lesson. Sometimes in life, as Christians we might be hard to please, and so God might use other method to teach us. God prepared a goad and made it come over Jonah so that it might be a shadow over his head, and to deliver him from his grief." Jonah was very glad for the goad. The following morning God prepared a worm that "smote the goad that it withered." God then prepared a strong wind "that beat upon the head of Jonah, that he fainted, and wished in himself to die." Jonah said it was better for him to die than to live.

God saw Jonah wearing the mask of self-pity, and God asked him, "Doest thou well to be angry, for the goad." The first time Jonah was asked a similar question, he did not answer, but this time he had an answer, "I do well to be angry even unto death."

When we are wearing a mask it is difficult to see the good things that God is doing. When we are wearing a mask it is difficult to see the love that God is demonstrating to others, and to us. When we are wearing a mask it is very easy to give up and allow self to take over. Yes Jonah was angry. Yes Jonah was wallowing in self-pity, and it was now time to take the mask off. God had the first word, and now God has the last word. God had displayed "His mercy and compassion to the Ninevites," and now God is proclaiming "that concern to every creature, both man and animal."

We serve a merciful and compassionate God, and we cannot hide from God no matter how hard we try. In

Jonah 4: 10-11 God closes the book of Jonah with these final words, "Thou hast pity on the goard, for the which thou had not laboured, neither madest it grow; which came up in a night, and perished in a night. And should not I spare Nineveh, that great city, wherein are more than sixscore thousand persons that cannot discern between their right hand and their left hand, and also much cattle?"

Jonah was wearing the mask of self -pity, but God had the final word to speak to Jonah. When God speaks we are called upon to listen and to obey the voice of God. I believed Jonah listened, and took heed to the voice of God, and removed the mask of self-pity. Thank God masks can be removed.

QUESTIONS AND COMMENTS

Jonah disobeyed God's voice. Why is it so easy to disobey God's voice?

....

....

....

Jonah was swallowed up by a great fish, and in the belly of the fish he cried out to God. Do you believe Jonah was sincere when he cried out to God?

....

....

God had showed mercy to an entire nation, but Jonah became angry and wanted to die, why?

....

....

....

☺ ☺ ☺ ☺ ☺ ☺ ☺ ☺ ☺

SCRIPTURE
MATTHEW 26: 69-75

PETER

TAKE OFF THE MASK

❀ ❀ ❀ ❀ ❀ ❀ ❀ ❀ ❀ ❀ ❀

CHAPTER 8

THE MASK OF DENIAL (PETER) TAKE OFF THE MASK

When we hear the name Peter, we readily think of the Apostle Peter one of the first disciple called by Jesus to follow Him. When we hear of the Apostle Peter we think of greatness, and one who was determined to be faithful to our Lord. When we hear of the Apostle Peter, we think of one who was willing to die for our Lord. This great man Peter was told by His Master that he would deny Him, but Peter declared that this would never take place.

Sometimes in life we are determined to do what is right, but without the Lord on our side we will surely fail. Peter was told by His Master that he would deny Him, and I believe Peter meant what he said, that he would not deny His Lord. Peter had witnessed the mighty works of His Lord, and Peter meant it that he would not deny His Lord.

When Jesus was arrested, Peter was willing to fight, and he took his sword, and cut off the ear of the high priest servant whose name was Malchus, because he was willing to stand up for Jesus. This same Peter who appeared to be so dependable; this same Peter who was willing to die for His Master put on the mask of denial. Peter was told by His Lord that before the cock crows he would deny Him three times.

In observing Peter's life, we could not imagine that

❂ ❂ ❂ ❂ ❂ ❂ ❂ ❂ ❂ ❂

Peter would deny His Lord. So often we hear of Christians who have done something tragic and we wonder how this could ever happen. From all outward indication, everything seems to be going alright and then comes the sudden shock. It is said that, "The Apostle Peter is one of the great stories of a changed life in the Bible." When your life has been changed you are now a new person in Christ. Peter's life was changed, but here we find Peter putting on the mask of denial that he did not know His Lord.

Foe over three years Peter had walked with the Lord. For over three years Peter had sweet fellowship with the Lord. Peter had belonged to "the inner circle," which consisted of Peter, James and John. This man Peter came to a place in his life when he put on the mask of denial and said he did not know Jesus.

Peter was bold and was not afraid to accept challenges. It is said that, "The Apostle Peter may have been the most outspoken of the twelve apostles in Jesus' ministry on earth. He certainly became one of the boldest witness for his faith." The disciples were asked by Jesus, "But whom say ye that I am?" Peter boldly answered, "Thou art the Christ the Son of the living God." The disciples were on a ship in the midst of the sea, and the winds were contrary. Between three and six a.m. Jesus was coming to them "walking on the sea." The disciples saw Jesus walking on the sea, and they thought they had seen a spirit, and they cried out in fear. Jesus told them who He was and that they should not be afraid. On the boat was Peter, and Peter said Lord, if it is really you let me come, and Jesus said come. Over and over again, Peter had demonstrated his boldness, and his closeness to His Lord, but the time came when Peter put on the mask of denial, and said he did not know the Lord.

Peter had seen the dead raised back to life; blind

⊕ ⊕ ⊕ ⊕ ⊕ ⊕ ⊕ ⊕ ⊕ ⊕

eyes opened; lepers cleansed; the deaf being able to hear; the dumb being able to speak again, but this same Peter put on the mask of denial and said he did not know the Lord.

It is so very easy for us today to look back at what Peter did, and might even say I would never do that. It is so very easy to point the finger at Peter and wonder what was wrong with him. As we look more closely at ourselves do we sometimes put on that same mask of denial and deny our Lord? Do we always stand for what we believe despite what the consequences might be? When we are in a group and things are being said negatively about our Lord, do we keep quiet and refuse to speak out? Peter meant what he said, that he would not deny His Lord, but he did.

Wearing the mask of denial might seem an easy thing to do. We might get away misleading our friends at work; we might get away misleading our brothers and sisters at church, but how long can we wear that mask of denial without being found out? We can mislead people some of the time, but we cannot mislead people all of the time, somehow, somewhere we will be found out. Man sees things on the outside, because man looks on the outward appearance, but God looks in the heart.

Let the story of Peter be a challenge to all of us, and let us endeavor to attempt great things for God. Let's be an authentic Christian, not trying to please man, but endeavoring to please God in everything that we do. Yes Peter had failed God, but thank God his love was restored. Peter denied His Lord three times, but in John 21 verses 15 through 21 he declared his love for Jesus three times. **Verse 15**, Jesus said to Peter, "Simon, son of Jonas, lovest thou me more than these?" Peter replied, "Yea, Lord thou knowest that I love thee," Jesus said to Peter, "Feed my lambs." **Verse 16,** For the second time

☻ ☻ ☻ ☻ ☻ ☻ ☻ ☻ ☻ ☻

Jesus says to Peter, **"Simon, son of Jonas, lovest thou me?"** Peter replied, "Yea, Lord; thou knowest that I love thee." "Feed my sheep."

We all should be thankful that we have a forgiving God. Of the twelve apostles Peter was the most out spoken in Jesus' earthly ministry. He also became one of the "boldest witness for the faith."

This man who had denied his Lord and who was forgiven, could be considered the greatest and most prominent of the disciples. Church historians and church tradition has given reliable evidence that "the Gospel of Mark is actually the gospel of Peter." It is said that Peter "dictated his discipleship with Jesus to John Mark, who was a companion of his for many of the latter years of his life."

This man who had denied his Lord had a glorious ending. It is said that "in the days leading up to Peter's death almost all of the apostles had been martyred." Peter who was regarded as an "arrogant, cocky, man of thunder," "became a humble, willing, obedient servant of the Lord even to death." Peter who had put on the mask of denial, had that mask removed, and rejoiced in that day of his death that he would be reunited with his Lord forever. Peter moved from a lowly fisherman, and became a mighty fisher of men. As Christians, that is our mission to be fisher of men.

<u>QUESTIONS AND ANSWERS</u>

Peter was not afraid to accept challenges, but he denied His Lord. Why do you think this might have happened?

....

....

....

Have you ever tried to walk on water? That is impossible, but Peter did. Have you ever denied your Lord? that's possible, Peter did. Do you want to be like Peter, which Peter, the one before or after Pentecost? explain

....

....

.

....

....

....

Why do you think Peter was considered one of the greatest and most prominent of the disciples?

....

....

Take Off The Mask

....

....

☺ ☺ ☺ ☺ ☺ ☺ ☺ ☺ ☺

SCRIPTURE
ACTS 5: 1-11

⊙ ⊙ ⊙ ⊙ ⊙ ⊙ ⊙ ⊙ ⊙ ⊙

ANANIAS AND SAPPHIRA

TAKE OFF THE MASK

❂ ❂ ❂ ❂ ❂ ❂ ❂ ❂ ❂ ❂

CHAPTER 9

THE MASK OF PRETENSE (ANANIAS AND SAPPHIRA) TAKE OFF THE MASK

In the early church, the Christians were actively engaged in doing God's will. They were on a mission in helping all those who were in need, and they sold their properties and gave it to the church so that others would be blessed. When we give freely to the cause of God not expecting anything in return God will bless. If we give with the sole purpose of receiving, we will lose our blessing. In many of our churches today, people are giving to a cause with the sole purpose of receiving a reward. We should not give to get blessed, but we should give because we are already blessed. It is good to sew seeds with the expectation of receiving a harvest so that everyone can be blessed from that harvest.

In the Jerusalem church, there was a couple, Ananias and Sapphira; they were impressed as to what was happening in the church. Many believed and "were of one heart and one soul." Many sold their possessions, and brought the prices of the things they had sold and laid it at the apostle's feet. Ananias and Sapphira saw an opportunity to put on a mask of pretense, and follow what the others were doing.

As Christians, we can pretend all we want, but God sees our heart, and sees behind the mask we are

● ● ● ● ● ● ● ● ● ●

wearing. We can pretend that everything is alright, but God can see behind the mask of pretense, and know that things are not the way we portray it to be. We can give the impression that we are having a glorious time, and others might believe it, but God can see behind that mask of pretense.

Ananias and Sapphira came up with a plan that they were convinced that the church folks would not find out and they would be looked upon as truly caring for others. They sold a possession they owned, kept back part of the proceeds, and brought a certain part and laid it at the apostle's feet. They did not have to carry out their plan, but with their mask of pretense they thought they would be safe. They must have thought they could just blend in with the crowd wearing their mask of pretense and no one would find out.

Ananias and Sapphira planned their deceptive work together but Ananias first approached the apostles and laid the given portion at the apostle's feet. Ananias received the shock of his life when Peter saw behind the mask he was wearing, and ask him the question, "Ananias why hath Satan filled thine heart to lie to the Holy Ghost, and to keep back part of the price of the land?" Peter then went on to ask several more questions, "While it remained, was it not thine own? and after it was sold, was it not in thine own power? why hast thou conceived this thing in thine heart? thou hast not lied unto man." Ananias had no time to try and defend himself, but when he heard Peter's words, he fell down dead. The young men, who were standing by, wrapped him up, carried him out and buried him.

Ananias was dead and buried, and his wife Sapphira had no idea what had taken place. She might have wondered what had happened to her husband, but after three hours had passed by she came and laid her given

😊 😊 😊 😊 😊 😊 😊 😊 😊 😊

portion at the apostle's feet. Peter asked her a very simple question, "Tell me whether you sold the land for so much?" She answered, "Yea, for so much." Sapphira just like her husband had worn the mask of pretense. Sapphira just like her husband had to suffer the consequence. Peter then informed Sapphira what had taken place by asking the question, "How is it that ye have agreed together to tempt the Spirit of the Lord? He then informed her that the ones who had buried her husband were at the door, and would carry her out.

Just like her husband, Sapphira had no time to try to defend herself, but when she heard Peter's words she fell down dead, and she was taken out by the young men and was buried. What happened to Ananias and Sapphira was a great lesson, and demonstrated to the church back then and to us today that we have to come clean before God. As a result of what had taken place to Ananias and Sapphira, the Bible says, "And great fear came upon all the church, and upon as many as heard these things.

It seems today in many of our churches people are playing games with God. It seems many have forgotten that God can see behind any pretense that we might try to be involved in.

☻ ☻ ☻ ☻ ☻ ☻ ☻ ☻ ☻

QUESTIONS AND ANSWERS

Why did God kill Ananias and Sapphira for lying?

....

....

....

Did Ananias and Sapphira believe that they could really fool God?

....

....

....

Putting on a mask in order to be deceptive can be very dangerous? What do you think?

....

....

....

☺ ☺ ☺ ☺ ☺ ☺ ☺ ☺ ☺

<u>NOTES</u>

• • • • • • • • • •

CHRISTIANS

TAKE OFF THE MASK

CHAPTER 10

DO CHRISTIANS WEAR MASKS? IF SO, TAKE THEM OFF

Do Christians wear masks? If so, as Christians, we are asked to remove the mask. Some years ago, I was listening to a Christian radio station, and the speaker was talking about **"Bogus Christianity."** The word bogus means, "not genuine or true, fake." The speaker was saying that there are Christians that are bogus, not genuine, not true, false, and not authentic. They look like Christians, they talk like Christians, but deep down they are not who they claim to be.

There are many around us who views Christianity in the wrong way. They have the strange idea that it is an easy way to get some money. Many years ago while I was employed on the U.S. Naval Base at Guantanamo (Gtmo) Bay, Cuba, we started a Christian Fellowship called, "The Jamaican United Christian Brethren Fellowship." We were Christians from various churches in Jamaica, and the idea was to come together and have Christian fellowship. We were very serious in what we were doing, and many accepted our Christian standing. There was a young man who was not a part of our group, and as far as we know he never accepted Christ as his Savior, but he was very articulate. So often as Christians, when we see someone who is very articulate, we try to give them the idea that they should be a minister. This young man came up with the idea of going back to Jamaica to start his own church. As far as I know we never heard what became of this

young man.

There are many bogus or false Christians around us wearing a mask and we should be aware of them. The Bible says in 1 Samuel 16: and the last portion of verse 7, "for man looketh on the outward appearance, but the Lord looketh in the heart." As Christians we should know God's word for ourselves, so that we will be able to detect false teachings when we are confronted with it. There are many who are wearing the name tag of being a Christian, but are not.

The Bible speaks out against false Christians or those Christians who are wearing a mask thus concealing their true identity. Here are some Bible verses that speak out against false Christians that are wearing a mask:

1. Matthew 15: 8: "These people honor me with their lips, but their hearts are far from me."

2. James 1: 26: "If anyone considers himself religious and yet does not keep a tight rein on his tongue, he deceives himself and his religion is worthless."

3. Titus 1: 16: "They claim to know God, but by their actions they deny him. They are detestable, disobedient and unfit for doing anything good."

4. 3 John 1: 11: "Dear friend, do not imitate what is evil but what is good. Anyone who does what is good is from God. Anyone who does what is evil has not seen God."

5. Luke 6: 46: "Why do you call me, Lord, Lord, and do not do what I say?"

☻ ☻ ☻ ☻ ☻ ☻ ☻ ☻ ☻ ☻

6. John 14: 23-24: "If anyone loves me, he will obey my teaching. My Father will love him, and he will come to him and make our home with him. He who does not love me will not obey my teaching. These words you hear are not my own; they belong to the Father who sent me."

7. 2 Corinthians 5: 17: "Therefore, if anyone is in Christ, he is a new creation, the old has gone, the new has come."

8. Matthew 7: 3-5: "Why do you look at the speck of sawdust in your brother's eye and pay no attention to the plank in your own eye? How can you say to your brother, 'Let me take the speck out of your eye,' when all the time there is a plank in your eye? You hypocrite, first take the plank out of your own eye, and then you will see clearly to remove the speck from your brother's eye."

9. Matthew 12: 34: "You brood of vipers, how can you who are evil say anything good? For out of the overflow of the heart the mouth speaks."

There are many false Christians who are expecting to go to heaven, but unless a genuine change has taken place from the inside out that will not be possible. Here are a few quotes from an article on "Fake Christians." **"Don't let your lips and your lives preach two different messages." "Your most powerful testimony is how you treat others after the church service is over." "What a heartbreak it would be to live an "almost" Christian life, then "almost" get into heaven."**

Take Off The Mask

● ● ● ● ● ● ● ● ● ● ●

Do Christians wear masks? Do choir members wear masks? Do deacons wear masks? Sometimes on a Sunday morning there are people who could be confused not being sure if they are in the right company, because there are so many around them that are wearing masks. There are people who knows how to blend in a church group, and who knows how to put on their mask and be a good actor. They know how to praise the Lord just right in their acting. They know how and when to say amen. They know how and when to say praise the Lord and Alleluia. In a church service that might last for two hours they know how to behave with their mask on, but if the service should go over the allotted time that is a different story. Isn't it strange how some Christians will go to a sporting event, and time is not a problem, but on a Sunday morning in a church service time is a problem?

Do some Christians wear mask? How do some Christians behave at work? Can people around them know that they are truly Christians or are they walking around with a mask? As Christians we are supposed to let our light shine before men, we are supposed to let our behavior be pleasing to God at all times, we are supposed to be different than those who are engaged in a worldly lifestyle. When someone sees us as Christians they should be seeing the "real thing."

It is Sunday morning and you have to go to church service no matter how tired you might feel because it is part of your life-style. Before going to church, there are two things you have to take, your bible, and your mask. It is at church that many do their spiritual gymnastics, and then on the rest of the week the mask is taken off, and they are back to normal.

Over 50 years ago when I was employed at the Naval Base in Guantanamo Bay, Cuba, my coworker informed me that some of his friends would go to the dance, get all

the latest dance moves and bring it to church. Even though I do not dance, there is nothing wrong with dancing if you are glorifying God with the right motive. Times have changed, I am old fashioned, but it appears today we are taking the world into the church, but whatever we do as Christians we should make sure we are doing it to the glory of God. So often as Christians we put on the mask, and call what we are doing by a different name. As Christians we are called to be authentic and live a holy Christian life, and not hiding behind a mask.

QUESTIONS AND ANSWERS

Why do Christians wear mask? Do you wear a mask, and if so can you identify the mask you are wearing?

....

....

....

Who do you consider to be a bogus Christian?

....

....

....

If you are a Christian, how can someone be able to tell that you are a Christian, and that you are not wearing a mask?

....

....

Be Yourself

☺ ☺ ☺ ☺ ☺ ☺ ☺ ☺

<u>NOTES</u>

THE MASK OF FAMILY MEMBERS

TAKE OFF THE MASK

❂ ❂ ❂ ❂ ❂ ❂ ❂ ❂ ❂ ❂

CHAPTER 11

THE MASK OF FAMILY MEMBERS TAKE OFF THE MASK

How are things going with you? Everything is fine and could not be better. Is that always the truth? Is everything always fine? It is so very easy to say things without really thinking of what is being said. It is so very easy to tell someone I am praying for you, but is that always the case? You see a brother or a sister who is having a rough time, and not knowing what to say, you may say, "you are looking good." The brother or sister knows what you say is not really correct, but you just don't know how to take off the mask and be authentic.

The story is told of a young girl who was taught by her mother to tell the truth at all times. Telling the truth was part of her lifestyle. The mother had run into some hard times, and was unable to pay her bills on time. The mother knew the bill collector would be coming by, and so she told her daughter when the bill collector comes by to tell him she was not at home. The bill collector came by, knocked at the door and asked the daughter for her mother. The young girl did not say her mother was not at home, but she said, my mother says to tell you that she was not at home. This girl was authentic, and she did not put a mask on to cover things up, but she spoke the truth.

Telling the truth should at all times be the lifestyle of a Christian. People should not be guessing if what you said was the truth or not. Christians should be trustworthy in the things that they do, and not be walking around wearing a mask.

A few months ago I was asked to speak at a men's prayer breakfast on the topic, ""Men Walking in Integrity." When men are walking in integrity, there is no mask to take off, but everything that is done is authentic. Allow me to share with you something that I said at the prayer breakfast. **"It seems that all over America and yes, in the church people are lacking in integrity. It is said that, "Integrity is one of the most misunderstood and misused words in organizations." It seems that there are many who think it is alright to lie, it is alright to cheat, it is alright to be unfaithful, it is alright to gossip, but God wants us as men to walk in integrity, and be consistent in our walk."**

It has been said that we all wear masks, but is that really true? What is everyone trying to hide? I tend to believe that not everyone wears a mask; I believe that there are many people who are authentic in the things they are doing. So often we all try to make a good impression, we try to be the very best we can, and sometimes it might give the impression that a mask is being worn. If we know that we are wearing a mask, it is best to take it off, and be yourself. My former pastor in Jamaica, W.I. many, many years ago spoke on the topic "Be Yourself." My pastor has been passed and gone for many years, but his sermon still lives on, and we are called to take off the mask, and be ourselves.

Someone has said that we all wear mask, but we do not have to accept it as being true. If we are in deed wearing a mask, we should endeavor to take it off and be ourselves. People have the idea when they see others they are not really the same as they are behind closed doors. I remember as a young Christian I was talking to

my coworker about the Lord. My coworker believed what I was saying, but he said he would have to see my life at home to determine if I was really genuine. What my coworker was saying is, that there are many who demonstrate a good life on the outside, but at home that is a different story, and this happens all the time. The mask has to be taken off so that our true selves can be revealed.

I would like to encourage all family members, wives, husbands, children, grandchildren, uncles, aunts, cousins, that if you are wearing a mask to take it off, and be yourself.

QUESTIONS AND ANSWERS

As a Christian do you find yourself lying to get out of a jam? If so, what are you planning to do about it? Will you take off the mask of lying?

....

....

....

Should integrity be the lifestyle of a Christian or should we just blend in with the crowd?

....

☻ ☻ ☻ ☻ ☻ ☻ ☻ ☻ ☻

....

....

Do you find it difficult telling the truth or do you sometimes have to think about what you should do? Can others trust you in the things that you say?

....

....

....

....

....

Did you find it difficult answering the above questions?

....

....

....

😊 😊 😊 😊 😊 😊 😊 😊 😊

<u>NOTES</u>

THE PULPIT AND SUNDAY MORNING MASK

TAKE OFF THE MASK

● ● ● ● ● ● ● ● ● ●

CHAPTER 12

THE PULPIT AND SUNDAY MORNING MASK
TAKE OFF THE MASK

The pulpit is a very sacred place, but it is a place where there are many mask wearers. It is possible for a preacher to be out on Saturday night, "doing his own thing," not sharing the word of God, and then on Sunday morning attempt to preach the word of God. It appears the sacred pulpit is used for many to develop an acting career.

I remember many years ago of a well known preacher saying how he was taught in seminary how he should act on the pulpit. This preacher said he did his act for many years, but he came to realize even though he was loved by many, all he was doing was acting. He decided to stop his acting and allow God to completely change his life, and it was then his ministry was completely changed. This preacher came to realize that he had to take off the mask, be himself, and allow God to take control of his ministry.

So often in our pulpit, and in our churches people are taking God's name in vain. As a result of this, when someone says "thus saith the Lord," we are apt to believe and say that God has spoken. I remember some years ago I was in a certain state, our pastor had retired, and we were praying and fasting for God to send us a pastor. One night after our prayer and Bible Class, a woman

☻ ☻ ☻ ☻ ☻ ☻ ☻ ☻ ☻ ☻

came off the street and informed us that God had sent her to pastor the church. Just hearing someone says, that God says to tell you would make someone wonder. It is true God might give someone a message from the outside for the church, but one would wonder why God wouldn't tell us Himself. There are many out there who are wolves in sheep's clothing, and when there is no under shepherd, no pastor, they will try to come in and take over, and so we have to be very careful.

So many pastors and ministers are ministering for the wrong reason. For some it might be fame, for some it might be fortune. We have heard of so many ministers and pastors who have failed in their ministry because their focus was not on God. The world is making fun at the church, because there are so many who are wearing masks, and not being authentic in the things that they do.

As Christians we are called to proclaim the good news of Jesus Christ, but so often we are hearing bad news of those who have failed along the way. We listen to the news, we read in the paper, and over and over we hear the bad news of preachers who have failed along the way. Despite all the failures around us, thank God there are those who are still proclaiming the word of God without mask.

Here are a few examples of what's happening around our world of preachers wearing a mask. In the **Christian Post** we read, "Pastor impregnates 20 members of his congregation and claims the Holy Spirit told him to do it." "The pastor claims to be obeying prophetic/spiritual injunction to do the will of God, which is to impregnate any one chosen and revealed by the Holy Spirit, irrespective of whether the woman is married or not."

In a religious article **"listverse,"** it is stated that, "Evangelical Christianity is often characterized by its preachers' flamboyance and charisma and their focus on

❀ ❀ ❀ ❀ ❀ ❀ ❀ ❀ ❀

entertainment and supposed acts of God over traditional churches more somber sermons." It has been stated that among the showbitz and the glamour, "a few preachers have lost their way and become embroiled in scandal." Here are a few descriptions on some of these preachers, "men like......whose tearful confessions have become infamous." Men "whose anti-gay sermons were rapidly discredited when it became clear that he had employed the service of a male escort..." Further investigations into this preacher's "personal finances and the finances of ministry revealed that he had been siphoning off large proportions of the money donated by his followers into his own bank accounts." This preacher "was sued for fraud by some who had sent in prayer requests in the genuine belief that he would be able to help and his television show was thrown off the air. Though his ministry still preaches it never came close to reaching the heights it achieved during his prime."

Many of these preachers have started out doing the right thing, but somehow along the way they have changed courses and started doing wrong. This preacher "was a big name in faith healing circles......with his television show being broadcast nationally in the United States." It is reported that "the shows generally took the form of...calling people out of his audience and apparently using his connection with God to decipher what ailments they suffered before laying his hands on them and providing the cure." This particular scam worked for many years and it made this preacher very rich."

It has been stated that this preacher "was not like any other evangelical preacher." He dressed like a hippie and maintained the look throughout his career. Furthermore he admitted that he struggled with homosexual urges, but he claimed that his work with the

☻ ☻ ☻ ☻ ☻ ☻ ☻ ☻ ☻ ☻

church helped him to eradicate them." It is reported that this preacher, "ran a successful ministry in his homeland....His main claim to fame was his supposed ability to produce "miracle babies" for .....couples struggling to conceive."

Christian preachers are called upon to live an upright life, a life set apart to do the Master's will. When preachers are living a life of affluence, and not helping those who are in need, then it is time to take off the mask. When Christian preachers are called upon to live a life pleasing to God, and are doing that which is contrary then it is time to take off the mask. When Christian preachers are doing what they think is right, and not doing what is right, then it is time to take off the mask. When Christian preachers can curse off their brothers and sisters, and go on the pulpit and pretend all is right, then it is time to take off the mask. When Christian preachers are not reaching out to those who are lost, then it is time to take off the mask. When Christian preachers are just being great actors, and does not demonstrate their love for others, then it is time to take off the mask. When Christian preachers are ready to fight at the slightest provocation, and will even kill if they think it is necessary, then it is time to take off the mask.

I remember as a young boy in Jamaica, my pastor who was a policeman said if someone broke into his house if necessary, he would kill. That sounds like a policeman talking who has been trained a certain way. I could not fully understand the idea of taking a life. Recently I heard a minister from the pulpit saying, if someone broke into his house in the early morning, he would realize that was not a friend breaking in, and he would defend himself even by killing. Sometimes we cannot give a suitable answer as to what we would do if confronted, but there is one thing we should remember

that vengeance belongs to God, and that God will fight our battles for us.

QUESTIONS AND ANSWERS

What is God expecting of you as a pastor/minister in the way that you live?

....

....

....

As a pastor/minister are you exempt in living as a Christian should?

....

....

....

Can you as pastor/minister do whatever ungodliness you want to do, and forget about living a holy life?

....

....

....

Take Off The Mask

As Christians, as pastors/ministers we are accountable to God, and God expects us to live an upright Christian life based upon His Word. If we are wearing a mask, that is preventing our light to shine, it is time to take off the mask, and let our light shine.

● ● ● ● ● ● ● ● ● ●

CHAPTER 13

SOMETHING TO THINK ABOUT:

LET'S ASK OURSELVES THESE QUESTIONS.

How can we teach others how to love when we are unloving?

How can we teach others how to pray when we do not pray?

How can we counsel others, when we are in need of counseling?

How can we tell others how to train their children when our children needs training?

How can we have a plank or a beam in our eye and is able to see the speck in our brother's eye?

It is time to take off the mask and be ourselves.

How can we tell others to be honest when we are robbing God and telling ourselves it is alright?

How can we tell others to walk in integrity, when our walk is in need of improvement?

☻ ☻ ☻ ☻ ☻ ☻ ☻ ☻ ☻

How can we tell others to be respectful when in our Christianlike way we are slandering others.

How can we tell others to make an effort to be in the house of God on a regular basis, when we feel contented in attending "Bedsde Baptist/Pillow Presbyterian?"

Hello Bro. John, I missed you in church today, where have you been? I am sorry deacon, but I took a little trip to "Bedside Baptist Church."

It is time to take off the mask and be ourselves.

How can we tell others not to lie, when every chance we get we are telling lies.

How can we be patting our brother on the back and say we appreciate you, and then go behind his back and talk negatively about him?

How can we say we are on our way to heaven, but we do not recognize Jesus is the only way?

How can we say we love the Lord, when we fail to do what He has asked us to do in His word?

It is time to take off the mask and be ourselves.

How can we say we love our family, when we fail to spend quality time with them?

☺ ☺ ☺ ☺ ☺ ☺ ☺ ☺ ☺

How can we say we are doing the best we can, and when a genuine need arise to help someone we refuse to help?

How can we say we care about others, but do not care when a need arise?

How can we say, "we are all one in Christ Jesus," when sometimes we are putting our brothers and sisters into classes, the upper class, the middle class, and the lower class?

It is time to take off the mask and be ourselves.

How can we say no sin can enter heaven, when sometimes as Christians our lifestyle does not show a mark difference from the non Christians?

How can we have this world's good, and see our brother in need, and shut our bowels of compassion from him?

It is time to take off the mask and be ourselves.

◆◆◆◆◆◆◆◆◆◆◆◆◆◆◆◆◆◆◆◆◆◆◆

● ● ● ● ● ● ● ● ● ●

OTHER THOUGHTS
"LET'S GO BACK TO THE GREEK."

Sometimes as preachers we might try to be impressive; and in so doing may give the wrong impression. It is wonderful if you have studied Greek and Hebrew; but if you have never studied Greek, what is the purpose of saying, **"let's go back to the Greek."** Is it a way of telling your listeners that you have added information, and that what is in The King James Version of the Bible is not good enough for our time? **It is time to take off the mask and be ourselves.**

I know of a minister who is self taught and that is alright, but he likes to use the expression, **"let's go back to the Greek**," **or "this is what it says in The Greek."** There is a preacher that I knew who taught Greek in seminary, but in all the times I have heard him preach, I never heard him say **"let's go back to the Greek."** On the pulpit we are not there to impress others, but we are there to preach. On the pulpit we are not there to make a name for ourselves, but to lift up the name of Jesus. On the pulpit we are not there to outshine our brother or sister, but to shine for Jesus, so if we are wearing a mask we should take it off and be our self.

◆◆◆◆◆◆◆◆◆◆◆

PROFOUND STATEMENT

At the closing of a recent church service that I

☻ ☻ ☻ ☻ ☻ ☻ ☻ ☻ ☻ ☻

attended, the speaker made two profound statements which I would like to share. He said, "Leadership is always about service and never about power." "Service is about ministry to others and not about controlling others." It seems to me in so many churches there are leaders who wants to have all the power, and the ability to control others. They want to be sure others know that they are "the big boss." It is time to take off the mask, and be humble as we deal with others.

◆◆◆◆◆◆◆◆◆◆

IS THERE A DOCTOR IN THE HOUSE?

Many years ago I was in a setting where there were many individuals using the title of doctor which was alright, until someone in the audience became sick, and the question was asked, "Is there a doctor in the house?" The person did not ask for a medical doctor, but simple, "is there a doctor in the house?" I don't believe there was a medical doctor in the house, but nobody responded. This might seem a bit funny, but maybe someone should take off the mask. At another setting I was in a meeting, when a brother's name was called. This brother has an earned doctorate degree, but refused to answer to being called brother, and in a very demanding way said I am doctor so and so, it is time to take off the mask. The Bible says in Proverbs 16: 18, "Pride goeth before destruction, And a haughty spirit, before a fall."

◆◆◆◆◆◆◆◆◆◆

BE YOURSELF

Take Off The Mask

I heard a young preacher who was preparing for ordination said, when he preaches, he does a little bit of this, (using a famous preacher's name) and he does a little bit of that, (using another famous preacher's name) and then he said, he will be himself. It is time to take off the mask, and stop being somebody else. God is looking for authentic Christians, and not bogus Christians to declare His word at all times, and to be himself.

WHAT HAVE YOU GAINED BY GOING?

Going to revivals is a wonderful thing; going to conventions and camp meetings is a wonderful thing; meeting friends and loved ones is a wonderful thing, but if we are not changed and challenged for the better, what have we gained?

In camp meetings; in revivals; in conventions; meeting friends and love ones, we blend in with the crowd, and sometimes we are wearing a mask, thus hiding our true identity. Friends and love ones might be wondering what is wrong, but with the mask on it is hard to determine.

PREACHING ABOUT SIN MIGHT BE UNPOPULAR

It seems to me that many preachers today are not preaching too much about sin, because the prosperity

gospel is more popular. It is time to take off the mask, the Bible is still true, "For the wages of sin is death; but the gift of God is eternal life through Jesus Christ our Lord."

♦♦♦♦♦♦♦♦♦♦♦
WHY WORRY? JUST TAKE OFF THE MASK.

Whitley Hopier contributing writer of crosswalk.com gave a report on Dr. Julianna Stattery's book, Beyond **the Masquerade: Unveiling the Authentic You.** She said that, "If you're in a hurry, you may not worry about leaving the house wearing a stained shirt or mismatched socks, without brushing your hair or putting on makeup. But what if other people could see beyond your physical appearance and look at your insecurities, pride, shame or malicious thoughts?"

Those are the things our society urges you to cover up. After awhile, you create masks to hide your true thoughts and feelings and present an image you hope will prove your worth. The longer you wear your masks, the more comfortable they feel. But you can't enjoy healthy relationships unless you remove the masks and show others who you really are."

She gave the following reasons of how you can take off the masks you present to the world and be authentic:
"**Realize the price of the masks you wear.**" It should be understood that your masks prevent you from experiencing intimacy with God. Rather than trying to impress God, pursue an honest and intimate relationship with Him while trying on His strength. Know that your masks prevent you from pleasing God. Instead of vying for other people's approval and praise, live to please God

☺ ☺ ☺ ☺ ☺ ☺ ☺ ☺ ☺

alone-no matter what others think of you. Shift your focus from establishing your identity on earth to becoming a disciple of Jesus."

◆◆◆◆◆◆◆◆◆◆◆

ASK JESUS FOR HELP

Nelson Price in his sermon, "It is time to take off the mask," writes, "Jesus Christ delights in helping people remove their masks. He lived among persons whose life-style was a charade. They, like many today, lived life as play-actors."

◆◆◆◆◆◆◆◆◆◆◆

❀ ❀ ❀ ❀ ❀ ❀ ❀ ❀ ❀ ❀

TESTIMONIES OF WEARING A MASK

In "The Ministry Mama," dated November 12, 2013 in an article entitled "The hidden dangers of Christians wearing a mask." Here is a portion of the testimony, "In my life after being called to ministry at 12 years old I found out as the years progressed that it was not popular in my high school to say that I was going to be a missionary. I began to reject the goody-goody label. Eventually after many yo-yo decisions of being convicted about wrong lifestyle choices making a U-turn back to God, I began down a slippery slope.
My excuses became, "it's too hard to go against the flow," and "I am just not strong enough." My goody-goody mask came on at church and certain friends covering my fleshly desires and sins. My "this is who I really am" mask covered my Christianity among my worldly peers. In both cases I was wearing a mask....just like everyone else that claims the name of Christ and acts worldly."

◆◆◆◆◆◆◆◆◆◆◆

A PASTOR'S WIFE

Testimony of a Pastor's wife as recorded in "Celebrating Pastors in Recovery." This is a very lengthy testimony, but here is a very small portion of the testimony. "As long as I can remember my family went to church. My uncle was the pastor, my father was a deacon and my mother was the Sunday school secretary of our small neighborhood church. I loved church so much; I would

pretend and play "church" just like I would play "school" or "dolls." Church attendance was an activity I never questioned. We were there whenever the doors were open. I'm thankful for the opportunities I had as a child learning truths from the Bible that my aunt taught me in Sunday school. My interest and love for music was encouraged and nurtured. Even though it was small, my church was an extended family that loved me very much.

At home, though, we lived out secrets that were never mentioned at church. On one side of the coin was a family who were founders and pillars of a church and on the other side were secrets of verbal abuse, affairs, sexual abuse, lies, alcohol and drug abuse."

Thank God for His grace and mercy, and this pastor's wife was able to remove the mask and said, "I don't want to pick the mask back up again. I want to be exactly who God has created me to be."

It is wonderful to know that the God whom we serve is a mask remover, and we do not have to be hiding behind a mask, but we can be our self. "What a mighty God we serve."

◆◆◆◆◆◆◆◆◆◆◆

In "The Christian Perspective Magazine," dated February 24th, 2018, Kate Hannon related a story of a girl who was wearing a mask. She said that on the outside this girl looked "like she had it all together." She always had a beautiful smile because she was wearing a mask. "It was easy to look put together wearing a mask." No matter

how this girl felt out of place on the inside, she realized that her mask was always smiling. "No matter how bad the sickness from which she suffered was, her mask was always looked healthy and vibrant."
She had a lot of problems by wearing a mask. One major problem, the mask kept her from getting better. Underneath the mask, this girl was suffering from "a terrible illness," and the mask kept her from getting the necessary help. Since no one around knew she was sick, I guess it was alright with her.

This girl came to the conclusion that she could not "handle the mask any longer," she needed help. Reluctantly she allowed a friend to see under her mask. She was surprised her friend was not alarmed, and she pulled up her own mask revealing that she too was trapped in an illness inside. For the first time they were honest with each other, and were able to help each other to get the treatment they needed. What a great feeling this was for them when they allowed the mask to fall off.

What a wonderful thing to let the mask fall off, and be yourself. You and I will be of no help to others, if we keep the mask on.

♦♦♦♦♦♦♦♦♦♦♦

☻ ☻ ☻ ☻ ☻ ☻ ☻ ☻ ☻ ☻

EPILOGUE

Adam and Eve disobeyed God's command and realized that they were naked, and tried to hide behind fig leaves, but from the very beginning man realized that he could not hide from God, and has to come clean, and remove the mask.

What is a half lie? A half lie is a lie, and Abraham must have thought it was alright to say Sarah was his sister, and not say she was his wife. Sarah was in deed Abraham's sister, but his half sister, and she was also his wife. Abraham's intent was to deceive, he had lied, and he had to take off the mask.

Jacob was a trickster, and he deceived his blind father in believing that he was Esau, and so received the blessing that was intended for his brother, and he had to take off the mask of deception and change his way of thinking.

Moses was the prince of Egypt, and was headed for greatness, but this was interrupted when he had to put on the mask of running away, because he had killed an Egyptian. After forty years of running away, Moses had an encounter with God, and he had to remove the mask. When one comes into the presence of God. you will not be the same anymore,

David was the king of Israel, he was considered to be a man after God's own heart, but he had to wear the mask of unfaithfulness when he committed adultery and murder. David continued to live as if nothing had happened, but one day his sin was pointed out to him, and David had to take off the mask. In Psalm 51 David cries out to God for mercy and asked for His forgiveness. As Christians we do not have to wear a mask, but we can have the mask removed.

Be Yourself

☻ ☻ ☻ ☻ ☻ ☻ ☻ ☻ ☻ ☻

Elijah had seen the mighty hand of God, but he put on the mask of hiding because there was a death threat on his life. Elijah was praying to God to take away his life because he was not better than his father. The mask of hiding was removed from Elijah when he submitted to God's will. Sometimes as Christians we might think we can escape the hands of God, but there is no escape. David writes in Psalm 139: 7-9, "Whither shall go from thy spirit? Or whither shall I flee from thy presence? If I ascend up into heaven, thou art there: If I make my bed in hell, behold thou art there." No matter where we go or try to go, we cannot hide from God,

Jonah knew God was a merciful God, and decided that he could disobey the voice of God, and flee from the presence of God. Jonah failed to realize that no one can flee from the presence of God because God is everywhere. Jonah had to take off his mask of self-pity, and surrendered himself into the hands of God.

Peter had walked with the Lord for over three years, and he had made a promise that he would be faithful to Him under all conditions, but he denied Him, saying he did not know Him. Peter had to take off the mask of denial, and repented for what he had done. Peter was sincere when he said he would not deny his Lord, but he failed.

Ananias and Sapphira were followers of the Lord, and they wanted to do what the others were doing. They put on the mask of pretense and tried to deceive Peter. They had the opportunity to take off the mask, but they refused to do so, and had to pay the consequences. Pretense can bring very serious consequences, so let's be true in everything that we do, because God knows all about us.

Do Christians wear mask? Thould not, but some do. As we listen to the radio, as we hear the news, as we surf

☻ ☻ ☻ ☻ ☻ ☻ ☻ ☻ ☻ ☻

the internet, we find out that there are Christians wearing the mask of deception. The Bible says in 2 Peter 2: 1-2 "But there were false prophets also among the people, even as there shall be false teachers among you, who privily shall bring in damnable heresies, even denying the Lord that brought them, and bring upon themselves swift destruction. And many shall follow their pernicious ways; by reason of whom the way of truth shall be evil spoken of." Many are deceived by the actions of these false prophets and false teachers, and so we have to know God's word in order to avoid these deceptions.

Great men have come and gone, and their names still lives on. There are infamous men who have come and gone, and are still remembered for what they have done. When you and I are gone, will we be remembered? All the time we have is now, so if we are wearing a mask let us take it off and be ourselves. Let's be the best we can for the Lord so He will be able to say, "Well done......"

If this book has been a blessing to you, there are two words you should remember, and share with someone....

BE YOURSELF

◆◆◆◆◆◆◆◆◆◆◆

☺ ☺ ☺ ☺ ☺ ☺ ☺ ☺ ☺ ☺

ADDENDUM

There are Christians, who talk a great talk, but the walk does not match the talk, and as a result, they should take off the mask. When the mask is taken off, one will show up their true self. If you are a drug addict and you are wearing a mask, when the mask is taken off it will show you are really a drug addict. If you are an habitual liar, and you are wearing a mask, when the mask is taken off it will show who you really are, a liar. If you are lacking in integrity and you are wearing a mask, when the mask is taken off it will show the real you lacking in integrity. If you are a gambler walking incognito in your mask, when that mask is taken off it will show your true self. Just supposed you won a million dollars playing the lottery while wearing a mask, surprise! surpise! would you take the mask off, and reveal your true self? I heard a very dedicated, respected minister said that she spend only one dollar buying the lottery. That is something to think about. Just recently there were churches involved in a LGBT march, they were not speaking against it, but they were supporting the march, and it is time for Christians to speak out, take off the mask, and be true to their convictions. God is calling for Christian men, women, boys and girls to be true to God in everything that we do, so that when others sees us, they will see Christ living in us.

◆◆◆◆◆◆◆◆◆◆

Take Off The Mask

TAKE OFF THE MASK

Take Off The Mask

☺ ☺ ☺ ☺ ☺ ☺ ☺ ☺ ☺ ☺

BE YOURSELF

● ● ● ● ● ● ● ● ● ●

TESTIMONIALS

"I Just read your book, "Take off the mask." It is an excellent read, and it's the very thing that I used to teach in my chemical dependency counseling career. In fact there was a poem that I used to use that was titled, MASKS. Theory is we start putting on masks at birth and by the time we reach adulthood we have worn so many mask that it is hard for us to know who we really are. It takes years of counseling and to peel off the layers of false identity and to be all God created us to be. Many times that's only a scared little boy trying to figure out life as he goes. Thanks for your significant contribution. Much love and God bless."

-REV. KEVIN M GOODE, SENIOR PASTOR, CHURCH OF THE HARVEST CHURCH OF GOD.

"This book gives spiritual insight and is a thoughtful provoking publication; a reminder of many individuals from my past. In my book, "Redeemed, Restored, Set Free," I wrote of an encounter I had with a young man who pretended to love me, proposed to me and married me only because his doctor told him to try marriage in order to hopefully change his affections toward men. I was his victim. In this case, my story was as painful as some of the stories in "Take Off The Mask."

Wearing the mask is not beneficial to anyone. Numbers 32: 23 says, "Be sure your sin will find you out" (KJV). No one can live a lie always. Eventually the mask has to come off. It may not come off when we would like it, but

☺ ☺ ☺ ☺ ☺ ☺ ☺ ☺ ☺ ☺

it will come off. God is all seeing and all knowing at all times.

As a pulpiter, there has been times when my assignments conflicted with my feelings. As a leader. persecution by others is of no small consequence. Subsequently, my mask has been to keep my personal feelings about some of my audience quiet to benefit the whole of the audience with the love of the Lord rather than speak from personal feelings. In an experience, I heard clearly, "Don't use my pulpit for your personal stuff." From that experience, I was cured. A famous quote coined by William Shakespeare, "To thine own self, be true." Though not from a Christian perspective, Mr. Shakespeare wrote words that can easily be ascribed to us all."

-REV. LINDA BRAGGS, ORDAINED MINISTER, CHURCH OF GOD (ANDERSON, INDIANA) AUTHOR, REDEEMED, RESTORES, SET FREE.

"Excellent job on your release: Take Off The Mask. I always love it when sermons and writings connect the Word of God to our everyday realities. You achieved exactly that by pointing out how various heroic trailblazers had to unmasked in spite of their fears of inadequacies, they completed the assignments the Lord had them to do. What a powerful life lesson for us to embrace. Also, the thought-provoking questions, which you included, helps us to examine ourselves for any hidden cover ups. Once again, an excellent read. Much appreciation."

-DR. PAULETTE J. BOSTON, AUTHOR OF "PAULETTE TALKS FAITH," A TRAVELLING ORDERS PUBLICATION.

☻ ☻ ☻ ☻ ☻ ☻ ☻ ☻ ☻

"This book is a spiritual experience, and the kind of knowledge you receive from Pastor Thompson cannot be duplicated elsewhere."

-FRANK AMBROISE, JR. AUTHOR

"The best book to break the mask of concealment due to inward fears. For God has not given us the spirit of fear, but of power, and of love, and of a sound mind. 2 Timothy 1: 7."

-PASTOR LAURENE NORMAN

❀ ❀ ❀ ❀ ❀ ❀ ❀ ❀ ❀ ❀

ABOUT THE AUTHOR

Derrick M. Thompson, Sr. was born in Jamaica, West Indies, the second of five siblings born to Luther and Floribel (Mable) Thompson now deceased. He is married to the former Isolyn Dennis of Jamaica, and they have three children, Karen, Derrick, Jr. and Duvol. They have three grand-daughters, McKale Lauryn Irie; Kori-Lynne Irie and Parker Yve, and a grand-son Graham Quinton. Derrick is an ordained minister of the Church of God with head office in Anderson, Indiana. He is a retired pastor, and served for eighteen and a half years as the senior past of the First Church of God in Harvey, Illinois. He is currently serving as an associate minister of The Solid Rock Community Church of God where Rev. Dr. Matthew A. Quainoo is the senior pastor, and Bishop Whitfield D. Blenman is the pastor emeritus. He received his early education in Jamaica. He has a Bachelor of Science in Accounting from Dyke College in Cleveland, Ohio; a Master of Divinity from Christian International Graduate School, and a Doctor of Ministry from International Bible College and Seminary. He was a doctoral student of Trinity Theological Seminary-Trinity College of the Bible. He is listed in the third edition of "Marquis Who is Who in Religion." He wrote his first book in 2013, "Take A Walk With Me," his second book in 2014, "Retired But Not Forgotten," and two more books, "Something To Think About," and "Sermon Summary 2016." Books are available on Amazon and on Barnes & Noble.

☻ ☻ ☻ ☻ ☻ ☻ ☻ ☻ ☻

BOOK RELEASE ON OCTOBER 18TH, 2019 IN MEMORY OF MY MOTHER WHO PASSED AWAY.

(OCTOBER 18TH, 1906 -APRIL 22ND, 2008)

Be Yourself

Take Off The Mask

142